Gift Of Graces

A Novel Based On Fact

Jane M. Spiotta

ISBN: 978-1-936539-51-2

Cover illustration by Tess M. Reardon-Walter

Cover design by Deb O'Byrne
www.redwillowdesignstudio.com

Book design by Chris O'Byrne
www.ebook-editor.com

Acknowledgements

First and foremost I want to thank God for his words, for giving me the determination to write them, and for giving me the strength to trust him through everything.

I am grateful for all of the "Graces" in my life — not only the divine Graces, but the woman, Grace, all true gifts.

Thanks to my husband, Gene, for all his love and encouragement since I have known him. To my beautiful children: Paul, Annie, and Tommy. To my mom and dad, brothers and sisters, and their spouses and children. Thanks for all of the love and support. My dear friends, you know who you are, I wish I could name everyone. Love to my precious Philomena, Lucy, Cisco, Joseph, and Bobby.

To Howard, who believed in my writing years ago. Marty, our conversations in P.E.I. helped inspire me to begin this journey. Melissa, who gave me the guidance and confidence to continue. To Rebecca, for taking the time to read the first draft, for your objective and professional opinion, and for the advice that helped improve it. To Tommy O., for his legal advice.To Nanc, for her voice whispering in a loud way to finish.

My editor, Chris O'Byrne. You are incredible. So professional, patient and kind. You were able to smooth out my writing, while still keeping my voice — not to mention the thousand questions you answered for me.

Tess, your artwork for the cover is perfect. I know how much time and love went into that painting. Thanks for sharing your gift with everyone. Deb, your design for it fit perfectly.

Eilleen, thanks for the photo shoot! Not only did you do a great job, but the memories of those hours will stay with me forever.

Last but not least, a great big thanks to Michelle, Grace's daughter, for faithfully calling me every week for years to make sure I was working on my book, and for being my constant cheerleader! Love you, my darlin!

The name *Anne*, meaning *grace*, is the traditional name of the Mother of the Blessed Virgin Mary.

Part One

Deliverance

The decision to be completely honest weighed heavily on my heart and mind while writing Part One. Protecting myself was not my intention. I am known well for wearing my heart on my sleeve. My life has always been an "open book", no pun intended. I did, however, wish to protect the innocent people in this story.

The reader should know that I feel no shame anymore. What was meant to be is what was. I believe that good can come out of all difficult situations, if not to ourselves, to someone else. We just need to have trust.

How I got myself into this situation need not be described, but the young reader must know that an insecure teenage girl, a teenage boy, and alcohol do not mix—ever!

Take whatever you need from Part One. My hope is that your heart will know what the real truths are...as you read.

For Mary Grace, Nola, Michaela, and Marylou.
"I am divinely guided to my right place."

Chapter One

A September Evening 2006

I walked down the hallway with the same emotionally fatigued feeling I had nearly every evening. As I entered the steamed-filled bathroom, I noticed the message my daughter Gracie left for me in the mirror. "I love you mommy, Love Gracie." I smiled recalling some of the innocent, but not as endearing notes I would leave for my sisters in my youth.

I shut the door behind me and locked it, as I wanted no intruders; this one half hour soak is all I asked for. While undressing, calm already began to take over me. It could have been the scent of the lilac bath oil, or just knowing the next 30 minutes belonged to me. Whatever the reason, I was grateful for it. I placed my jeans and sweater onto the closed toilet seat; carefully I submerged my toe into the tub of steaming water. "Ah perfect", I thought as I slithered the rest of my 5-foot 6 body into the bath. Resting my head on the back of the tub, I began to take my typical surveillance of the bathroom. The salmon colored tiles were really getting to me, especially the cracked ones, which rested above the tarnished faucet. The molding around the frosted window, which had sporadic puddles of mold on it, was painted white. This bathroom definitely needed to be redone. The peaceful feeling I had began to leave me, so I quickly glanced over at the framed photo which sat on the back of the toilet. It was a picture of my daughter Gracie and niece Erin, with arms around each other, their faces stared back at me with beaming smiles on them. I'd wondered if they knew how much joy they brought me. I then let my eyes wander to the shelf above that cherished photo to probably the most precious material possession in my life. It was a rose, given to me by my sister Grace; pale pink and of a silky material, it rested in a pretty white vase. Next to it was a sand dollar (which by the way, was part of my inspiration for writing this book) that was found two years earlier on a beach somewhere in Canada. As I followed the circumference of the sand dollar with my eyes, I thought about the idea of my life coming full circle. Sliding myself down, submerging myself deeper into the water I closed my eyes to remember. I remembered...

Twenty Two Years Earlier

This bathroom was much prettier; after all, my sister Grace decorated it.

Grace was a wonderful decorator, which came last to her church and family obligations, and next to last to her studies, which she always excelled in. In my mind there was nothing Grace didn't excel at, with the exception of holding her not-so-great temper now and then. Of course, that's not to say she ever hurt anyone with her occasional outbursts, on the contrary, they often made whoever was around one, giggle. Poor Grace. I stood in the newly renovated room. Red and blue calico print wallpaper covered the walls. A typical white commode sat next to a matching pedestal sink, which had remnants of dirt left in it by my nephew Michael. Looking into the oval shaped mirror above it, I hardly recognized the person staring back at me, and truthfully didn't want to know her. I lifted my T- shirt to just expose my midriff. Turning to the side I studied my belly's profile in the glass. " I don't see any difference in it yet?" I thought. I then began to go over the dates in my head.

"Maybe I have the dates wrong, yeah, right, wishful thinking."

"Jane, Jane," I heard bellowing through the house. I could tell it was Grace's voice coming from the kitchen. "Jane."

"I'll be right there," I hollered back.

Quickly pulling my shirt down and taking a deep breath at the same time, I found my way to the kitchen. The kitchen, it was Grace's dream kitchen. It was quite large. The walls were painted a cranberry red, which complimented the knotty pine cabinets. An island sat close to the center of the room. Behind it was the table family meals were shared around. This kitchen even housed a fireplace. Grace said it was one of the deciding factors for her when opting to purchase the home.

I stood in the entrance of the "Grande room," to find Grace sitting at the table, her face in a book (not an unusual way to find her). The hard covered book in her hand read "Anatomy 2". Grace was a nursing student, dedicated wife of Tim, devoted mother of four: Michael 12 years of age, Bethany

10, Marie 7, and Barbara 3, respectfully.

I stood watching Grace, having so much admiration for her. Even with the serious and intense look she had on her face at that moment, she still looked pretty. Her brown wavy hair framed her chiseled face; her almond shaped pale green eyes matched the blouse she was wearing. With shame for doing so, I envied her ambition and the expectations she had of herself.

"I guess it wasn't urgent, huh, Grace."

She looked up at me with only her eyes. "Oh, hey, Jane, I'm sorry for shouting from in here. I'm so involved in what I am reading here, I don't want to walk away and lose focus. I just wanted you to check on the girls for me, they're upstairs playing."

"Sure, no problem," I replied with little enthusiasm.

"You okay, Jane?"

"Yeah sure, just a little tired."

"Did you get your period yet?"

I often wondered why Grace made every mood or emotion pertain to "that time of the month". She did, though, and she knew my monthly cycle better than I knew my own.

"Nope, not yet."

With that answer, Grace completely lost focus and actually put her book down.

"You're not pregnant?"

"Yeah, right. With whose baby?" I answered with quite a bit of sarcasm to sound believable.

"Just checking. It is odd, though. You're never late, and it's been about two weeks now, right? If it's okay with you, I'm going to make an appointment for you with Dr. Jacobs, okay?"

"Sure, whatever you think."

"I'll call tomorrow," she replied, and proceeded to put her face back in her book.

I then walked through the spacious and well-decorated living room, which was equipped with a second fireplace, and walked up the stairs to the girls' room. I poked my head into the bedroom. Three single beds covered in pink gingham spreads lined the wall. Marie was lying on her back, her hair in disheveled braids underneath a baseball cap. She was throwing a ball up in the air and catching it in the mitt on her left hand. Bethany sat studying as intensely as her mother. She was sitting at an old maple desk Grace had purchased at an antique shop that she and I frequented. Bethany was so much like her mother and looked just like her. With the same dark hair and pretty green eyes, she even had her mother's temper. We'd giggle at poor Bethany, too. I then looked over at Barbara who was sitting on the floor in front of her blue wooden dollhouse. She was playing ever so contently.

"Hey, girls, what's up?"

"Oh, hi, Aunt Jane," replied Bethany. "Nothing much, just doing my homework."

"Nobody will play catch with me," whined Marie.

"Maybe I will after dinner," I told her.

I glanced over at Barbara who was pretending to feed one of her dolls. I don't think she even noticed I had come into their room. I wouldn't dare disturb her; she looked so content taking care of her baby. Baby, I thought, not a baby. I dismissed the idea immediately, something I had done every day for the last two weeks. "I'll be downstairs if you need me, girls. Don't disturb your mom, she's studying. Oh, and Marie, we have a date for a catch after dinner."

Marie turned to me and smiled. "Thanks, Aunt Jane."

I had a catch with Marie that evening and retired to my room early. I was able to call it my room because Michael kindly turned it over to me. He did so without much resistance. After all, he took over the den that came equipped with a television. My room was on the main floor, which was adjacent to the living room. Because it was originally Michael's room, it had a rather masculine look to it, as it should. Moth's wing colored paint covered the walls and blue and brown scotch plaid curtains hung from the windows. A solid navy blue throw rug lay on top of the full-size bed. All of the furniture was dark wood, like new. Yes, it was a little boyish for my taste, but it was warm and cozy, and for the time being, I could call it mine.

After setting my alarm clock and saying my prayers, I climbed into bed quite exhausted. I turned off the lamp and then laid there wide-eyed. Many thoughts invaded my mind. *If Grace takes me to the doctor, she'll find out for sure. How* will I explain? I was a good girl, or so Grace thought, and I know my parents did as well. I began to pray again, "Please, God, take this away from me now and give it back to me in the morning." Followed by, "How about you just take it away from me all together and just leave it at that." I felt guilty for saying it, for thinking it. The guilt covered me, and then I drifted off to sleep.

Chapter Two

The sound of cars buzzing by and the scent of lilies that were growing outside the screened windows woke me up before my alarm had a chance to ring. The scent brought me back to my childhood: sitting on the front stoop of our family's home with the other neighborhood children. I could hear my mother humming from the kitchen window; the faint sound of a baseball game my father was watching echoed from the living room. The scents and sounds from childhood; there is nothing quite like them. Reality quickly crept back in as the pretty scent of lilies abruptly changed to a foul odor that made me sick to my stomach. After mustering my queasy self out of bed, I put on my size-six blue jeans (those were the days) and an old t-shirt. I then began to tie my infamous bright orange sweatshirt jacket around my waste. As I did, little pieces of hay fell from its pockets to the floor.

ॐॐ

I worked for the YACC (The Young Adult Conservation Corp); at a place called Emmet Farms. It was an exhibit farm open to the public. Local schools brought their young classes there on field trips, and you would get an occasional family with small children visiting once in a while. Anyway, I was the least likely of the nine children in my family to work on a farm, as I wasn't known for being a big animal fan. Besides, I never wanted to be dirty. I took the job because it was the only one I could get after spontaneously moving in with my sister Grace and brother–in-law Tim. I eventually began to like the job, especially because of all of the people I worked with. There was Shana; she was the manager of our crew. She was a tall, pretty brunette who shined with confidence and kindness. Susan was her assistant, another tall brunette with short hair. When I first met Susan she was reserved, but very sweet. It didn't take long for us to become friends. John, Steven, Karen and Ellen made up the rest of the crew, all lovely people to work with. They're the ones I worked alongside every day. I

guess you could say we did the dirty work; cleaning out cow
stalls, pig pens and chicken coops. We also fed the animals,
milked the cows, and even bailed hay, which was the most
germ-free chore of the day and the one I liked best.

I have to say the highlight of my experience working there
was that we had the privilege of working alongside the AHRC.
(Association for Handicapped and Retarded Citizens). They
worked on the farm with us, but in a different area, doing the
gardening out in the many acres of fields. I looked forward
to seeing them every morning and then again at lunchtime.
They truly were the joy of my day, which was a surprise to me.
From the time I was a little girl, I was always afraid of people
that were "different".

Meanwhile, back in my room, I managed to pick up the
hay that fell on the floor in spite of the lightheadedness I
was feeling that morning. I made my way into the bathroom
to brush my teeth. While looking at myself in the mirror, I
brushed my waist-length dark brown hair into a ponytail. I
raced from there into the kitchen and grabbed the last bran
muffin off a plate that was sitting on the counter. I shouted a
goodbye to everyone, not even knowing if anyone was home,
and ran out the door to wait for my co-worker Karen to pick
me up. I still didn't have a driver's license or a car, so I paid
Karen a whopping 15 dollars a week to transport me to and
from work, and it was well worth it. It was a long walk from
Grace's, and there was no public transportation in that area.
Besides, it was door-to-door service. At 6:45, give or take a
minute, she would pull up in her light blue, 1970 Volkswagen.
Our journey to work was often awkward. We never really said
too much to each other. I don't know if it was because she was
so shy, or because we really didn't have too much in common
except that we lived in the same town and both bailed hay for
a living. At least for the time being we did.

We pulled into the grounds of Emmet Farms after an
almost completely silent ten-minute ride. I always got such a
warm feeling when we approached the farm; it looked like an
old painting, so imperfect, which in turn made it perfect. In the
center of the farm sat four structures that were surrounded by
about 15 acres of land. I would say at least ten of those acres

were just grass for the animals to graze on, and was the shade of kelly green—how I pictured Ireland's green to be! At least three of the acres were hay, and the other two were gardens of veggies of all types. Now, the structures consisted of an old farmhouse painted pale yellow. It had a lot of large windows and a white, wraparound porch. Both house and porch were in need of a few coats of fresh paint. It housed one family. A young couple, Doug and Barbara, who tended to the farm when we weren't there, which wound up being mainly on the weekends.

The first floor was used for the YACC and AHRC. It was split up into different offices for management. The only room we all shared was the kitchen, a rather bare space with the exception of a small 1950's looking fridge, an old farm sink, a waste basket, and a large kitchen table that we enjoyed our breaks around. Three barns also sat on the property; one was whitewashed stone and the other two were red and framed in white. That was where the cows, sheep, goats, and pigs lived. The chicken coop was set up closer to the fields where the AHRC worked.

As I stepped out of Karen's car, the odor was so overwhelming; I could hardly bear it. It's mind over matter, I kept telling myself, it's mind over matter. I quickly walked over to the farm house to get away from the stench. "I'll meet you in the stone barn in five minutes, Karen. Thanks for the ride!" I shouted. I couldn't get in the house fast enough. Feeling dizzy and nauseas, I swore I would lose the bran muffin I had just eaten for breakfast. After darting through the front door, I ran in the kitchen and leaned into the sink, turned on the faucet, and began splashing water on my face.

"Ah, you awhite, Jane?" someone grunted in a deep, husky voice. It was Billy and his entourage. They stood all in a row, staring nervously. As sick as I felt, I couldn't help but smile. I was touched by their sincere concern. "I am just fine gentlemen, thanks for caring about me." I winked at them, and Billy smiled back.

Billy was about five-foot three, a little heavy set, with chubby, rosy cheeks and slanted dark eyes. Billy had Down syndrome. He came to work every day dressed in a crisp white t-shirt and blue and white striped overalls, cleaned and pressed. He even wore an engineer hat to match his outfit. He made sure he tipped that hat every time a girl walked by — so cute and such a gentleman. At lunch time he would display his Snoopy lunch box in the middle of the dining table for everyone to see. Often when I looked at Billy I thought of his mother. What was it like to pack a grown man's lunch in a Snoopy lunch box? I pictured her ironing his clothes, laying them out for him to get dressed and then kissing him goodbye before he went to go on the bus, as if he were a little boy. I didn't know her, but I admired her and felt sorry for her at the same time. It was really how I felt for all of the parents of these men/boys. Yet, as bad as I felt for them, I knew all of these men must have brought their parents so much joy, as they did me.

Back to Billy. He clearly had a crush on me. In fact, he used to sing to me from the fields. "Jane, I love you, Jane." It was so sweet, but I had to be careful of what I said and did around him, because as much as I cared about him, I didn't want to encourage him.

Billy's sidekick at work was a fellow named Brian. He was a friendly guy, I'd guess about 30 years old. He had a neatly trimmed beard and a smile that covered half his face. "Do you ever stop smiling?" I'd ask. He would giggle, "Well, I guess if I'm not standing on the corner watching all the girls go by." He said that nearly every day, and I never got sick of it. Their lightheartedness and lack of ego is what made them so special. Billy tipped his hat at me and began marching out of the house with his buddies following. He started whistling to the tune "Hi Ho, Hi Ho, it's off to work we go". As I watched them leave the house, I couldn't help but think of what this world would be like if we were all without such intense egos. What a different world it would be. "See you at lunch, guys!" I shouted as I followed them out the door.

Typical chores took place that day. We cleaned out the pig pens, milked the cows, and even fixed a broken fence, which was my first and last attempt at carpentry. Smelly and exhausting pretty much described the whole day, along with some good conversation and a few laughs. Of course, Billy and his pals helped me get through it like they did nearly every day.

Upon arriving home that evening, I walked straight through Grace's mudroom into the laundry room, which conveniently had a shower. I was particularly dirty that night and didn't want to dispense the odor of manure and stale hay throughout the house, and I knew Grace and the family would appreciate it if I didn't.

I closed the door, disrobed, dropped my clothes to the floor, and stepped into the shower. I began to relax under the hot, hard streams of water when, once again and without warning, the word BABY popped into my head. Trying to avoid the thought of it, I lathered up quickly, rinsed off, and grabbed my pink terry cloth robe off a hook that I had hung there the day before, putting it on while dripping wet. I did all of that in what seemed like fast motion, hoping that somehow moving quicker would help me escape my thoughts. I raced through the kitchen and living room into my bedroom where I found Grace sitting on the edge of my unmade bed. "Hey you, how was your day, anything yet?"

I knew what she meant, so I looked at her trying not to appear nervous. "Wish I could say yes. Kind of weird, right?"

"For you, yeah, that's why I went ahead and made an appointment with Dr. Jacobs. The only opening he had was for this Wednesday at 4 o'clock. Any chance of you getting off a little early? I'll pick you up."

Immediately my stomach began to turn. "I'll check with Shana, it shouldn't be a problem."

"Good, otherwise we'll have to wait at least two weeks to get another appointment. I'd like to get you in there to see him as soon as we can to give us both peace of mind."

I walked over to the mirror and began to comb through my sopping wet hair. As I did, Grace stood up to leave the room. She abruptly stopped in the doorway and turned to me. Dinner will be ready in 15 minutes."

"Great, I'll be there in ten to set the table. Oh…and Grace?"

"Yes?"

"Thanks for caring so much, you know, for making that

appointment for me."

Grace smiled. "Sure, what are sisters for?"

As I stood before the mirror finishing my hair, I thought about how blessed I was to have Grace in my life. She was so caring and a person who took action, not a person of mere words. There wasn't anything she wouldn't do for another person. Sure, she was human. Complaints came, but seldom through her good deeds (usually because she thought she wasn't good enough or fast enough at whatever she was doing), but her heart was always in the right place. Thinking of Grace at that moment relieved some of my anxiety; I actually felt a little peace.

Dinner hour was about the same every night. Tim always seemed to enjoy Grace's cooking. Sometimes he'd be so busy eating he'd forget the rest of the family was there. Grace took that as a compliment. Tim was a good person, too, and always excelled in his work. He was extremely well-read. I think his collection of books had probably exceeded 500. Grace would proudly let people know that he read every one. I cared very much for Tim, even though he was quite the tease to anyone who was in his path. It never bothered me. On the contrary, it made me feel good. That was one of the ways he showed you he cared. He did it the same way 13 years earlier when he first came into Grace's and our family's lives.

Tim and Grace met in college, and according to Grace it was love at first sight. After a few months, Grace finally mustered up the nerve to invite Tim to our family home for a visit. Poor Tim walked into utter chaos and relentless pranks shelled out by my four older brothers. He surprisingly took them all in stride; it had to be hard to take, seeing that he was an only child. There were nine of us—a whole baseball team! Grace was the oldest, and then there was Bill. He was a handsome boy, and at the time Tim came, he was in his last year of high school. He worked at the local A+P and rode a motorcycle, which naturally didn't please my parents. Kathy came next. She was a year younger than Bill, and gorgeous, too. She was a bit of a rebel back then and had a slew of friends. She went out with the high school wrestling champ who she eventually married.

Before I continue with the description of the rest of my

siblings, I must say with the risk of sounding prideful, that being attractive was something none of them had control over. Even with each of their personalities being different, they all shared the same strength in character and integrity, a lot of which I credit my parents for.

Danny followed Kathy in line. He was tall and thin, with a great sense of humor. He was a good student, always a help to my mom...really a good boy. Tommy was the silent brother who didn't always show his mischievous side (later we found out just how mischievous he really was!). He was a carpenter, electrician, and plumber. Jack of all trades, master of all. He really was sweet, with broad shoulders and huge dimples.

As the youngest boy, my brother David had it the hardest. He had to be the tough boy in order to survive. He was often the comedian at my expense. In allowing him to do that, I take some credit for molding him into the fine young man he is today (just kidding), although he certainly is one of the finest! Tess was two years older than me. She was a straight-A student and great in sports, painting, poetry, and many other things. She carried those gifts into adulthood. Chrissie was my only baby sister. She was a bit of a tomboy, extremely funny, and cute. She was the apple of not only my parents' eyes, but all her older siblings' as well.

Dad was a World War II Veteran whose nickname was Sarge. He was an extremely hard worker and madly in love with my mother. He was strict, but with a playful side. He was grounded in faith and the importance of family and friends. Strong and warm, strict and playful, and ever so wise. All of that wrapped into one handsome man—my dad. I could never pay homage to my mother with mere words, but I will try. Her main goals in life were to please God, all who were around her, and herself last. Some might call her a martyr for always putting others before herself. I'd call her selfless and loving. She also happened to be one of the best piano players I've ever heard. Her beauty surpassed most, inside and out. An indescribable light, my mom. That's why thinking back to the day Tim came to our home for the first time makes me laugh, but when I think of what my poor mom went through it makes me want to cry!

There were several stories referring to that first infamous

visit to our home. What I recall was...

One afternoon, Tim was lying on my brother Bill's bed. He was reading, his head and back resting on a pillow against the headboard. Tommy climbed to the second-floor ledge outside of the house and waited while David sneakily and skillfully fed the garden hose up to Tommy. After sticking the end of the hose through the partially opened window, Tommy looked down at David and gave him the thumbs up. David then began to turn the water on while Tommy squeezed the nozzle on the hose, which was aimed right at Tim. Leaping and dripping wet, he found his way to the door and hid behind it screaming my mother's name. Unfortunately for him, she wasn't home. Fortunately for Tommy and David, he never ratted them out; at least not right away.

He was barely over that when my siblings fed him a story about a fire drill that we did weekly in our house. They made a map and gave it to him. They told him to study it and to learn his route out of the house because we would be having a drill that night. I'm sure he studied it; naturally there was never a drill. He probably stayed up all night waiting for it.

Poor, Tim. He was officially initiated into our family. As insane as it was, those pranks came with love, which I am sure he felt, and over the years he gave it right back to them!

Grace and Tim were married one year later. I recall their wedding reception, standing among the guests in my lavender dress with a black velvet bow in my hair—both sewn by my mother's hands. I watched as Grace and Tim waved goodbye to all of us. I wept and wept; it was a terrible moment for me. I always felt especially close to Grace who was like my second mom. Her moving away took its toll, which is why my parents let me spend a good part of every summer with Grace and Tim.

Now we're back at Tim and Grace's table. Michael was not enjoying the dinner in front of him, especially the peas; neither was I, peas being my least favorite food of all time. Michael didn't know it, but I watched him skillfully glide the peas off his plate with his fork to hide them under the rim.

"Are you doing anything tonight, Jane?" Grace asked.

"Uh, no definite plans. Why?"

"Tim and I were thinking of going to the movies."

Tim looked at me with a hint of pleading in his eyes.

"Yeah, thought I'd take your sister out on a date."

"Sure, no problem, but you little stinkers better listen to me. When I say it's bedtime, it's bedtime. Right, Mom and Dad?"

"Homework, baths, and bed," Tim said authoritatively, then glanced at me and smiled.

"First, Michael and I are going to do the dishes." I said while winking at him. "You clear the plates, okay, Mike?"

I despised peas myself. What kind of Aunt would I be if I let them know his little secret?

"Yeah, sure, Aunt Jane," he said, grinning.

Homework, baths, and bed was just how the evening went, but not without a few little arguments between Michael and Bethany — typical sibling rivalry. Finally, the children were nestled all snug in their beds. All the while I lay in my own bed with no thoughts of sugarplums, only thoughts of BABIES.

Chapter Three

Wednesday arrived much quicker than I had hoped. Grace and I walked into Dr. Jacobs's office. The waiting room was rather cold and dreary. Maybe it was just the intense anxiety I was feeling that made it feel that way. I filled out the necessary paperwork and waited to be called. A tall, stern-looking, redheaded woman poked her head out the door. She was middle-aged and wore wire-rimmed glasses perched on the end of her tiny nose, a nurse's dress, white stockings, and white shoes. She even had a little cap on her head that had a decal of a red cross on it. I hadn't seen a nurse dressed like that since I was a little girl. Her professional look was both surprising and intimidating.

"Jane Ross," she said straight-faced.

Grace looked at me and smiled. "Go ahead, it'll be okay. It'll be over before you know it."

I stood up and walked toward the redhead whose name tag said "Margaret". I looked back at Grace who gave me another sympathetic grin.

"Go ahead," she said. She knew how uncomfortable I was. I am sure she would have taken my fear away if she could have. Little did she know that the fear of the examination was nothing compared to the inevitable dreadful news I was about to hear; news that would change my life forever.

"Come this way," Margaret said, as she walked down the hallway toward another door. She held the door open for me while giving me a sort of smirk. Guess it was her smile!

I walked into the examination room and felt an intense chill. It looked and felt colder than the waiting room. The walls were painted a dismal gray, bare except for a red, metal medicine cabinet, a Norman Rockwell calendar, and a few muted floral paintings. She walked me over to a green, leather-topped examining table. It had metal stirrups at the end of it. I didn't know what they were at the time. Handing me a blue cotton gown, Margaret ordered, "Take everything off from your waist, down. Put this on with the opening in the front; the doctor will be with you shortly."

"Sure," I replied nervously. Margaret left the room.

As I was changing, I thought about how much I just wanted to find a way out of that office, to run and keep running from this nightmare that was officially about to begin. I finished changing, hopped up onto the examination table, and waited. Dr. Jacobs opened the door. He was of medium height and semi-bald with a slender face and kind eyes. He wore a lab coat with tan, corduroy pants and earth shoes. He didn't look nearly as threatening as Margaret. He actually looked rather gentle — not at all what I expected. He reached his hand out to shake mine. "Hi, I'm Dr. Jacobs," he said, smiling. "What brings you here, Jane?"

"Well, truthfully, I think I'm pregnant," I confessed with a shaky voice.

"I see. When was your last period?"

"I think it was about seven weeks ago. I can't tell my sister, she'll kill me."

"Calm down now, I'll check and see. Just put your feet in the stirrups and slide down to the end of the table."

"Okay." As I did, I saw a very odd-looking contraption in Dr. Jacobs' hand.

"What's that?" I shrieked. "Is this going to hurt?"

"It's called a speculum," he said as he pointed to the object in his hand. "It will be cold and slightly uncomfortable, but it won't be painful. Try to relax."

Biting my lip and squeezing the side of the table, I muddled through the exam.

"Well, your uterus is swollen, feels like you're a good eight weeks."

I could, but couldn't, believe what I was hearing. Completely numbing myself out, I heard the buzz of the doctor's voice, but couldn't really comprehend what he was saying.

"Jane, are you with me, dear?"

I finally came back to the moment. "Yes, Doctor, I'm so sorry. I'm scared." My eyes began to well up with tears. "What am I gonna tell my sister? I can't tell her here, now."

"I'm not going to say anything to her. You do, however, need to make a decision on what you're going to do about this pregnancy. You have only four weeks to terminate."

"How much will it cost?" I couldn't believe those words were coming out of my mouth. Abortion was something I felt so passionately against when it came to other girls having them. Now that it was me in that situation, it actually became an option.

Dr. Jacobs looked back at me with his arms folded. "If you have it in my office, it will run you about 800 dollars If you have it in a clinic, it will probably be 350 or 400." How sickening it was to hear that. It sounded like a business transaction, and here we were talking about a human life.

"Can I let you know?"

"You can't wait too long if you want it done here, it's not a simple procedure. We need to block out a good amount of time. You'll need to make an appointment within the next few days."

Dr. Jacobs left the room and closed the door behind him. I sat there on the edge of the examination table in that ridiculous gown, feeling traumatized, dirty, and scared to death. After cleaning myself up and getting dressed, I went out to the waiting room to find Grace reading one of those medical magazines.

"Hey, Grace, I'm finished."

Grace looked startled. "Oh, hey, that was fast. Well?" she asked with anticipation.

"Well, what?" I replied, knowing full well what she meant.

"What did the doctor say was the reason you're so late?"

We both began to walk toward the door to leave. As I held the door open for Grace, I blurted out, "Don't worry, I'm not dying! "

Grace stopped in her tracks. "That's not funny."

"I'm sorry, you're right. He said it isn't unusual for someone my age to miss a period now and then. He told me if I didn't get it in the next month to come back in for some blood work to test my hormones or something."

I was shocked at how quickly those words came out of my mouth.

"Oh, okay, does that make you feel better?"

I was relieved to see that Grace was satisfied with my

explanation. "Sure, I guess. That exam was no picnic, though."
Grace smiled. "That's nothing, wait 'til you have a baby."
I returned a forced a smile. As we walked back to the car,
my heart raced and my stomach turned with worry about
how I would get through the ride home without making the
anxiety I was feeling evident. Grace put her seatbelt on, put
the key in the ignition, and turned it. We were on our way.
Immediately, she turned the radio on. I watched her long
slender fingers push the buttons; once, twice, at least five
times before she finally found a song she liked: "American
Pie". I was happy it wouldn't be a silent ride home. Traffic
was heavy that afternoon, and Grace's air conditioning
was broken. As the heat rushed in the windows, so did the
sound of beeping horns and a loud roar from a caravan of
motorcycles behind us. While stopped at a red light, I looked
out the window. I couldn't help but notice how normal people
looked. There were two teenage girls crossing the street, both
of them petite blondes and carrying matching purses. It was
obvious they were having a pleasant conversation: one was
laughing as the other spoke. I followed them with my eyes
to watch them embrace two boys that were standing in front
of a Friendly's restaurant across the street. I felt such envy as
I watched them all walk into the restaurant together. Their
lives were so normal and they didn't appear to have a care in
the world. That was my life two months ago. As insignificant
as that moment might have seemed, it was when I truly
realized that the path of my life had taken a huge turn in the
wrong direction. All I saw was darkness in my future; — a no-
win situation. The light turned green and we continued our
journey home with Grace's pretty voice singing along with the
radio. As we pulled into the driveway, I could see Tim in the
distance driving his lawnmower. He spent every spare minute
he had manicuring their three acres of property.

It was no surprise that they decided to buy that place.
Although the kitchen might have been part of Grace's
motivation for moving there, the landscape and the two homes
that sat on it were definitely the big seller. A brick walkway
led to the first house. It was bright white with black shutters. A
slightly tarnished brass knocker hung on its hunter green door.

200 feet behind the main house was another home. It was much smaller and painted the same way, only the front door was black to match the shutters. It housed a young couple, and years later it would be my parents' home. Flower beds were everywhere. They grew all different types of flowers, I only knew the names of a few, but what I did know was that it looked and smelled like the Botanical Gardens. What a beautiful place to live.

My attention turned to Grace, once again, as soon as she turned the car off.

"I'll see you inside, I want to say hi to Tim."

"Sure." I smiled.

Grace dropped her keys in her purse, exited the car, then leaned into the opened window. "You coming?"

"Oh, yeah," I replied. "I'm going to sit outside for a while."

"Okay," Grace said as she walked towards Tim.

I got out of the car and walked over to the patio. It was a basic red brick patio furnished with an outdoor dining set, a few cocktail tables, and two green Adirondack chairs. I plopped myself in one of them, trying to come up with the best way to tell Grace I was pregnant. The reality was that there was no good way.

ॐ∙≪

Grace paced back and forth in a frantic frenzy while I sat on the edge of my bed, weeping. "How could you have let this happen? You're so irresponsible, and who's the father?"

I began to explain through my sobs. "Remember the weekend you went to Canada? Well, I went to a college party with Kris and his friends. I met a boy there; he was sort of a friend of Kris's. We were all drinking. I stayed at the dorms because I was afraid to come home and sleep in this house alone. We drank some more, and I sort of slept with the boy. I was wasted, and I know it was really stupid."

"I'll say it was stupid, and who is this boy? Does he know?" Grace asked angrily, as she continued to pace back and forth. "What are you going to do now? You have to have an abortion. Mom and Dad can't find out about this; Mom will

have a heart attack or Dad will have a stroke!" I looked up at
Grace. Her face was covered with blotches, and I could tell
by the way her hands were shaking and by the way her voice
sounded that she was beside herself. She stopped walking and
leaned up against the window sill. She hung her head down as
if she was feeling shame for me.

"I asked Dr. Jacobs about an abortion, he said it would
cost 800 to have it in his office and about 350 to have it in a
clinic."

"Well, you are not having it in a clinic. You'll have to get
the money from this boy."

"He doesn't have it, and besides, he wants nothing to
do with this. I refuse to beg him for help. It seems that this is
gonna be solely my problem."

I could hear Grace's breathing from across the room; it
was clear to see and hear how distraught she was.

"I don't want to tell Tim yet. He is so crazed at work right
now, and I don't want to put any more stress on him. We'll
have to figure out another way to come up with the money."
Silence filled the room for a long moment. I felt relief when
Grace finally walked toward me and sat down next to me.
Her trembling hands began to wipe my tears. "We'll work this
out," she said softly. "It'll be okay." She wrapped both arms
around me and gave me a tight squeeze. I gave her one back.
She stood up and walked away. I said nothing. I couldn't. I
eventually got up to turn the light off and made my way back
to my bed. I closed my eyes and curled my body into the fetal
position.

It seemed as though I had just closed my eyes when I
heard the pitter-patter of what sounded like big feet coming
from the floor above me. I slowly opened my eyes to find it
was already morning. I then noticed I was still wearing my
clothes from the day before. Somehow I found it easier to get
out of bed that morning. I'm sure it was Grace knowing my
situation that made the weight on my shoulders feel lighter.
I made it through my work day the same as the weeks prior,
feeling overly tired and sick to my stomach. Work was even
less enjoyable that day because my pal Billy wasn't there. Not
only was I concerned about why he wasn't there, but I missed
his happy spirit.

After I arrived home that evening, I showered immediately, as I typically did, and headed straight for my bedroom, which was where I found Grace. I couldn't help but think of how familiar this scene was becoming.

She grinned at me as I looked at her. "How are you feeling?"

"I'm doing okay, feeling a bit relieved now that you know."

"Well, I'm getting past the shock of all this. I even went to see Father Phil today."

"You did? Why?"

"Truthfully, I was praying about the advice I gave you about the abortion. It wasn't exactly sound advice. I gave it to you based only on my reaction to your shocking news. So, I decided to go see Father Phil. He told me to let you know that no matter what you decide to do, he's there for you if you need to talk to him. He also asked if you would take the time to read something for him, it's from the Bible. I'll leave it open here for you. You don't have to read it now, maybe you can before bed."

"But I don't want to read it; I know what it's going to say."

"Maybe later, Jane. Dinner will be ready in a few minutes."

I looked at Grace, feeling defeated. "Yeah, maybe later."

Later came much sooner than I had hoped it would. Before I knew it, everyone had gone to bed. It was just me in my room with the Bible and dead silence. I finally gathered up my courage and placed the bible in my lap. On a small piece of scrap paper, I read, "please read Psalm 23, verses 1 thru 4. Love Grace."

The passage read,

The Lord is my shepherd, I have everything I need. He lets me rest in fields of green grass and leads me to quiet pools of fresh water. He gives me new strength. He guides me in the right paths, as he has promised. Even if I go through the deepest darkness, I will not be afraid Lord, for you are with me. Your shepherd's rod and staff protect me.

I took a deep breath and read it again. I read it probably four or five times, then I shut the book. Shaking out of fear, I pulled the blanket from the end of the bed and covered my trembling body — even covering my head, as if to hide myself in shame. I closed my eyes and slowly drifted off to sleep.

There was a large, white cloud. It began to slowly separate in two from the center. There emerged an illuminating light that surrounded a woman. She looked fulgent and beautiful. She was clothed in a white gown, a blue veil covered her head and much of her body, and a crown of roses was above her head. She floated. I gazed at her in awe as an angelic gentle voice began to escape her mouth. "Do not be afraid, Jane. Please don't do it. I promise I will be with you through this."

The brightness forced my eyes to open. It was morning. It took me a while to realize what had happened. When it hit me, I immediately sat up. What I saw, what I heard — was it real? All I knew at that moment was whatever had happened during the night convinced me there was no way I was having an abortion. The morning dragged on at work, with not much happening. Billy was back though, and he sat next to me at lunch. As we ate, Shana started to delegate the afternoon chores.

"There's a whole lot of hay to be bailed. I think we have waited long enough for it to dry out after yesterday morning's rain. It may be a little heavier than usual. Do you think you can handle it, Susan?"

"Think so, Shana," she replied.

"How about you, Jane and Karen?"

"Of course," Karen said, looking at me.

Shana smiled. "Great. John, you drive the tractor, okay?"

"No problem," he said with a mouthful of food.

As I sat there chewing the last bite of my sandwich, I suddenly became very protective of this little life inside of me. As everyone got up from the table, I pulled Susan aside. "Susan, I need to talk to you for a minute."

"Sure, is everything all right?"

"Yeah, I just need to speak to you about something," I whispered.

Susan looked over at the rest of the crew who were walking towards the door.

"You guys go ahead, I'll meet you outside. Jane and I have something to take care of."

They all continued out the door; John looked back and gave us the okay sign.

Susan looked at me with concern. "Let's sit down, Jane, you look so serious."

"I'm sorry to say it is, and I don't want you to think ill of me." I began to cry once again.

"Oh, honey, what's wrong?"

As I looked at her, I could see the concern in her deep-set eyes, and she took hold of my hand. "I'm pregnant." I was surprised at my lack of subtleness.

"Hey, kid, it's okay. Does anyone else know about this?"

"My sister, Grace, that's it."

"What are you going to do?"

"I'm not sure. I do know that I'm not going to have an abortion. I'm a little afraid of lifting the hay. Do you think it could hurt the baby?" How ironic, I thought, yesterday I would have lifted a truck if I could. I would have done anything to end the nightmare I was in, but today was different; ever since that dream I just felt different.

While still holding on to my hand, Susan said, "I think we should tell Shana."

"We should?"

"Yeah, I think she's the ideal one for you to talk to."

"Why?" I asked, looking at her puzzled.

"You'll see." She pulled me up by my hand and said, "Come on, let's go." We walked through the kitchen and down the hallway towards Shana's office.

Shana was a wonderful boss with a dynamic personality. I enjoyed her company and admired her work ethic, but I couldn't, for the life of me, figure out why Susan thought she was the one I should be speaking to. We stood in the doorway of her office. It was rather small with eggshell colored walls.

They had what appeared to be family photos hung on them, and there was plenty of plant life that filled much of the room. Susan tapped lightly on the opened door. Shana sat at her desk writing intently, and looked up, startled.

"Oh, hey, guys, come on in. What can I do for you?"

"Sorry to interrupt. Jane needs to speak to you about something."

"Sure. Close the door, have a seat girls."

Susan looked over at me. "Would you like me to leave, Jane?"

"No, please stay," I replied nervously.

"What is it, Jane?" Shana asked with curiosity.

"Well, I shared something with Susan and she thought I should tell you."

"Okay."

"I'm pregnant." There was that lack of subtleness—again.

Shana let out a long sigh. "Well, there is good reason Susan brought you to me. I went through the same thing a year and a half ago."

Knowing she didn't have a child (at least one that lived with her), I said, "You don't understand, I don't want to have an abortion."

"That's just it, Jane, neither did I. I had a baby girl and gave her up for adoption."

"Oh, I see." I sat in shock for a moment. How could this girl sitting across from me be so happy, so normal, when she gave her baby away?

"I don't think I could give my baby to someone else."

"Honey, that's not a decision you need to make right now. The important thing is you made the decision to follow through with your pregnancy. Let's just take it one day at a time. I can help you, Jane. I'd like to help. When I was pregnant, I went to a wonderful counselor named Elizabeth. I'm still in contact with her. I have a few things to finish up here, then I'll give her a shout. I'll set up an appointment. She works in the city. I have no problem taking you to her."

"That would be great, Shana. Thanks so much." Susan looked at me. I could tell she was pleased with herself for bringing me to Shana, and I was pleased with both of them.

For the first time since this happened I felt a glimmer of hope. I even felt somewhat normal.

I could hardly wait to get home to tell Grace all that had happened since the night before. The intense dream I had, plus all that transpired with Shana. She actually had been in my position and was going to help me. It all seemed so miraculous to me. Everything that had happened in the last 18 hours had changed my outlook on everything. Where there was darkness was now a shimmer of light.

❧

"You'll never believe what happened after I read that bible passage last night. I read it several times and fell asleep. I had a dream. I think I saw the Blessed Mother."

"What? Slow down, slow down." Grace looked concerned, like she thought I was crazy. "What do you mean you think you saw the Blessed Mother?"

"I know it sounds farfetched, maybe a little nuts, but I saw her. She was beautiful, and she was surrounded in a bright light. She asked me not to have an abortion and told me that she would be with me. I'm telling you, Grace, I saw her. That's not all. I went to work and told Sue I was pregnant. She had me tell Shana. Shana shared with me that she had a baby last year and gave her up for adoption." I know I sounded like I was going in fast motion. I continued, "She had a counselor from the city, her name is Elizabeth. Shana is gonna call her. She really wants to help me. "

"Calm down, Jane. Speak slower. You're all hyped up."

"I'm sorry. I just couldn't wait to tell you. I wanted some of your burden to be lifted. I've done enough damage already. I don't want you to worry about me. Handling this on my own is important to me."

"Oh, Jane, I want to help."

"That goes without saying. You are always there for me. You have Tim, the children, and school to worry about. I got myself into this situation. I need to be the one to handle it."

"What about this boy?"

"I told you, he wants nothing to do with this. I'm not going to beg for his help. Truthfully, I am not sure I want anyone to know at this point, at least not until I decide what I'm going to do with the baby. You understand?"

"Of course I do."

We both breathed a sigh of relief and embraced.

Chapter Four

The lettering on the glass door read "Catholic Charities". Shana held the door open for me and a blast of cold air hit my face.

"Ah, that feels good," I said, feeling relief from the stifling heat we left outside. "You aren't kidding. There's nothing like good ol' AC after working a hot smelly day on the farm." We both giggled. We approached the reception desk, which had a sweet, young girl sitting behind it. I could tell she was sweet because she had a sincere grin on her face the entire time we were standing there — one that stayed on her face even when she spoke.

"Can I help you?"

I looked at Shana, waiting for her to answer. "Yes," she said, "we are here to see Elizabeth Sully."

"May I have your names, please?"

"Just tell her it's Shana and Jane."

"Oh, yes, you're a little early. I'll let her know you're here. You can have a seat."

We weren't sitting two minutes when a short and rather plump woman entered the waiting room. "Shana," she said loudly.

Shana stood up. "Elizabeth?"

They walked toward each other, both of them grinning from ear to ear. Elizabeth reached her short arms up to Shana's face and placed her chubby hands on each of her cheeks.

"Look at you, honey. You look as pretty as ever."

"Thanks, Elizabeth. It's so good to see you. I'd like you to meet my friend Jane."

Elizabeth turned her attention toward me. "Hi, Jane. It's lovely to meet you. Shana's told me a lot about you."

"Likewise," I said nervously.

"Well, let's go to my office and talk, shall we?" As we entered her office, Elizabeth plopped down into her chair. As I stood there watching, I couldn't help but notice that her feet were dangling in the air; they didn't even touch the floor. I looked up at her face. She was different-looking in a cute sort of way. Her pixie haircut suited her round face. Her makeup, however, was a little over done. She wore blue eye shadow, lots of rouge, and bright orange lipstick.

"So, Jane, have a seat. You, too, Shana.

"Shana has shared a few things with me regarding your pregnancy. I know you're not much involved with the baby's father, and that you want to have this baby."

"Yes, I do. I know Shana gave her baby away. I'm not so sure I want to do that. I'm not sure what I want to do with my baby."

Shana looked at me sympathetically. "You don't have to make that decision now, Jane, You have time for that. I thought for today we could talk about ways we could help you. Where do you plan on staying throughout your pregnancy? Shana mentioned you live with your sister."

"I do, but I don't want to stay with her. She has small children. Until I decide what I'm going to do, I think it's best if they don't know. I prefer telling as few people as possible, at least for now."

Elizabeth sat looking at me shaking her head as if in agreement. Shana stayed silent.

"What about your parents? Don't you think you should tell them?"

"I'd prefer to wait it if I can. I want to have things in order before I break this to them, if I break this to them. I don't want to tell them at all because I don't want to hurt them, and at the same time, I want to do the right thing."

Shana cleared her throat to get our attention. "Well, I was thinking. Jane, you know my plans for moving down south, right?" I nodded. I'm sure I looked pretty confused.

"Well, I'm leaving in September. I'm going down to Florida for school to get my Master's in Special Ed. Billy and those guys sort of inspired me. Anyway, I thought maybe that could work in your favor. You can tell your family you're moving with me. Send whatever letters you want to me. I'll send them to your family so they are postmarked Florida. Whatever they send to me, I'll send to you. I know it sounds sneaky, but if you feel that strongly about keeping it from your family for now, you can do that and still have the baby."

I sat there listening intently. She made it sound so simple and sensible, and yet it seemed so deceitful. Should I lie or upset my family? I was never much of a liar, but I was about to become one.

Elizabeth looked at me quizzically. "If you don't mind my asking, why don't you want to tell your family? Are you worried about them being angry?"

"Maybe at first they'd be angry, maybe even shocked. But I know without a doubt they would support me. I just feel I need to do this on my own. I've made such a mess of things." I began to cry.

Shana leaned over, rubbing my back. "It's okay, Jane. I know this is hard for you."

I looked up at Elizabeth, still half crying. "Do you have any suggestions on where I can stay?"

"Well, you have a couple of options. We can have a family sponsor you, or you can live in a home for unwed mothers."

"I don't have the money for that."

Elizabeth replied, "Don't worry about the money; we're an adoption agency, this is what we do."

"But, I told you I don't know what I am going to do with this baby."

"Shh, don't worry. We're willing to take that chance. We'll help you regardless of what decision you make. What I want you to do for now is to think about all that Shana and I have presented to you. In the meantime, I'll set up another appointment for you for a few days from now. We'll be able to talk more then.

❦

The rain was pouring down in buckets as we pulled up to Catholic Charities for the second time in a week. We entered the building, soaked to the skin. I looked at Shana. "I hope you know how much your help means to me."

Shana replied with evident sincerity. "You know I've been where you are. I know how essential support is to anyone in this situation. So many people helped me through it and I wanted to give back in some way. You are my chance, kid, so thank you!"

This time I walked into Elizabeth's office feeling much calmer. I even giggled at the sight of her feet dangling from her chair. I couldn't help it.

"So, dear, have you done a lot of thinking about things the last few days, or what?"

"Yes," I said, shivering. It was so cold in her office and I was drenched from the rain. "I'd still like to keep this quiet for now. I decided to go along with Shana's idea, you know, saying I'm moving to Florida. Hope you don't think I'm terrible."

"Although I don't think you are terrible, it doesn't matter what I think. If you feel it's the best way to handle this situation, then that is what you do. Have you made a decision on where you want to live?"

"I did. I think being with girls that are in my predicament might be helpful to me, as well as a little more comfortable."

Elizabeth stared at me, nodding. "That makes perfect sense, Jane. There's a place here in the city called Rachel Residence. It's an old convent, and it's run by nuns. It only opened a few months ago. So far we've gotten good feedback from the residents there. If you would like, I'll call to see if there's a bed available." Elizabeth reached for the phone.

"No, wait," I said frantically. "I'm not ready, yet. I'd like to stay with my sister for a while, at least until the end of September."

"Oh, all right. How about I reserve a bed for the beginning of October?"

Taking a deep breath, I said "Okay, October it is."

Chapter Five

With suitcase in hand, I walked out of Grace's house, letting the door slam behind me. While waiting for Grace, I once again took notice of the splendid grounds that surrounded me, thinking that when I returned to Grace's nothing would look or feel the same.

The leaves were already beginning to change to a rainbow of red, orange, and yellow. It was a rather blustery day, so the ones that had already fallen were now dancing across the paved driveway. I always delighted in the change of the seasons, especially winter to spring and summer to fall, when such beautiful changes took place. This particular morning it was a bit cold out, and the air smelled especially fresh. I took a deep breath, the first of many that day. It was D-day, and I was off to Rachel Residence. Our trip was another silent one. I didn't want to think, nevermind speak. I felt bad not talking to Grace, but I knew she understood. I stared blankly out the car window the entire ride into the city, watching the beautiful landscape turn into something that resembled a ghetto. I saw a big steeple in the distance.

"That must be it ahead. See the steeple?" Grace asked.

"Uh, huh," I replied without enthusiasm. "Looks kind of creepy around here, don't you think?"

"It'll be fine. You won't be out walking the streets; you'll be in the convent with the other girls, nice and safe."

Easy for you to say, I thought as we pulled into the driveway.

There were three buildings in all. The one with the steeple on it was the church. It was old, a little run down, but possessed its own charm. A brick building sat next to it, which I figured was probably the rectory. To the left of that was a tremendous house, which obviously was the convent. It had a wide set of cement steps that led to two large, red doors. A sign hung from one of them that said "Welcome to Rachel Residence". As we stood in front of the doors I could feel my stomach starting to turn, sort of like it would on the first day of school every year as a kid. I even had the same fears. What if I don't fit in, what if the girls don't like me? Before we had a chance to knock, the door opened up to a middle-aged woman with black-rimmed glasses and short, dark hair.

"Hi, I'm Sister Rita. Welcome. You must be Jane," she said as she gazed down at my belly. She was no doubt expecting to see a more swollen belly, but there wasn't much of one yet. Grace reached out her hand to Sister Rita. "Hi, I'm her sister, Grace. It's nice to meet you."

"Come on in," Sister said, holding the door open for us.

We stepped into a sizable foyer. In front of us was a wide carpet-covered staircase with an elegant dark wooden banister. To the right of the stairs was an enormous living room. It had a couple of weathered looking couches in it that were covered in flowered slipcovers. There were also a few chairs, none of the fabrics matched. The windows were huge, light yellow drapes hung over them. Pocket doors separated the rooms. It was a historic looking home, with one grand, inviting room after the other. Sister showed me the kitchen, which was the last room on the first floor. It was much more contemporary looking than the other rooms, and not as charming.

"This is our kitchen." She pointed to a bulletin board that was hanging on the wall. "That is where you will find chores for the week. Your name will be added to the list. Every week we switch off with the different tasks; from cooking to doing dishes, cleaning bathrooms, dusting, vacuuming, et cetera. There are enough of you girls here to delegate the chores to. Don't worry, you won't be overworked." She smiled. "Now I'll show you your bedroom."

After climbing the long stairway we made a right into a hallway that was painted a soft sky blue. Dark brown doors lined both walls on each side. The fifth door on the right was mine.

"This is your room." Sister stretched out her arm into the room as if to say, "Tada!" Wow, bright orange, I thought, not quite what I expected. As loud as the color of the room was, the rest of the room was simple. It had a tall oak dresser with a round lace doily on top. A single mattress covered in white sheets rested on a metal frame, a folded plaid quilt was at the foot of it. A crucifix hung above the bed, which gave me a sense of peace. I placed my suitcase and the rest of my bags on top of the bed.

"This will be fine," I said, smiling shyly at Sister Rita (Eventually the orange room and Sister Rita grew on me). "Where are all the girls?" I asked.

"Oh, they're on an outing with the other sisters, they went to a Harvest Festival. We try to get the girls out on weekends. I usually go along, but I stayed back to await your arrival."

"Oh, I'm sorry," I said.

"No need to be sorry, we're happy to have you here. Besides, I had a nice quiet morning," she giggled. "They should be back shortly. In the meantime, why don't we go downstairs and have a cup of tea? Grace, will you join us?"

"Sure. I can't stay long, but I'll sit with you for a few minutes. Thank you."

I gazed at Grace with fearful eyes. I didn't want her to leave me there. She knew it, but there was no choice for either one of us. Walking down to the dining room, I couldn't help but notice the scent that filled the air. It was so familiar; sweet, with a hint of staleness to it. Because it was familiar, it made me feel more comfortable, even though I wasn't sure what the smell reminded me of. Sister Rita led us to a one of the six round tables in the dining room and told us to have a seat while she fixed the tea. We sat opposite each other. I looked over at Grace, my foot tapping nervously.

"What do you think, Grace?"

"You'll be fine here. Sister Rita is so nice, and so is this house."

"But I'm really scared."

"I know it has to be scary; it's a new experience, and a difficult one, but you will be surrounded by caring people. It's just going to take some time, Jane."

She looked at me with a slightly pitiful smile. After a long moment of silence, I blurted out, "Grandma and Grandpa's house!"

"What are you talking about?"

She looked completely puzzled. "That's what this house smells like," I said, feeling quite satisfied that I figured out what the odor was reminiscent of.

Grace inhaled deeply through her nose. "Oh yeah, I know what you mean."

I could tell it didn't mean to her what it meant to me. She was going back to the sights and smells of her own home. Breathing in the scent of my grandparents' house helped me to feel more at home there. I held on to that to give me some comfort that day and for the duration of my stay.

No sooner did Sister Rita walk in with a tray of tea and cookies did we hear a door slam and the sound of several female voices fill the air. "Well, the troops are home," Sister Rita sighed, smiling at us.

One by one, the girls paraded in, all of them staring at me. Some were holding pumpkins, while others were holding nothing at all.

"Girls, this is Jane."

A round-faced girl with sable colored hair and big chocolate eyes stepped towards me. "Hi, I'm Maria."

Smiling nervously, I stood up and walked toward her. "It's nice to meet you. This is my sister Grace." Grace smiled at her. Just then, another girl stepped forward. She was dark skinned with braided hair and a beautiful bright smile.

"Hi, I'm Shannon." I waited for the rest of the six girls to introduce themselves, but they all just smiled and walked away, with the exception of one girl who grunted, sat down, and helped herself to my tea.

"Okay, I guess that's my cue to go," Grace said as she stood up.

"Oh no, please don't go." Sister looked sternly at the girl drinking my tea. "Elandra, that was extremely rude, please apologize to Jane and Grace."

"No really, that's okay; I have to get home to my own troops anyway."

"Well, it was nice meeting you, Grace. We promise Jane will be well taken care of."

"I have no doubt," Grace said.

"All right, then. I'll walk you to the door, Grace. In the meantime, why don't you say goodbye to your sister. Jane, Maria and Shannon can take you upstairs and help you get settled after you say goodbye."

I looked at Grace, teary-eyed, and shrugged in agreement.
Grace hugged me. "Oh, Jane, it'll be alright. I'll be back to
visit soon, and I'll call you tonight."

I wouldn't let go of her. I held onto her with all of my
might, taking notice of how frail she was. She eventually
broke herself free of my grasp. She kissed me on the cheek
and walked away, leaving me standing there with these
three strangers. Two of them seemed rather sweet, while the
third sat at the table finishing my tea. She, I felt very leery of.
Following Maria and Shannon up the stairs, I asked Maria
how long she had been working at the residence. She didn't
look pregnant, and had a rather mature look to her. Maria
looked at Shannon, both of them laughed.

"What's so funny?" I asked, feeling quite awkward.

"Working here? Honey, I'm one of you, or should I say,
you are one of us? C'mon, we'll help you unpack."

That's when I knew I would be okay. I had the smell of
my grandparents' house with me, and not one, but two new
friends. So what if my room was orange?

Night fell quickly. In my bed I lay on my back, staring
at the ceiling, with not much to look at but the moonlight
gleaming over it. You could hear a pin drop, the silence was
deafening. I couldn't sleep, so my mind kept wandering into
the future, fear and anxiety traveled with me. My heart raced;
I could practically hear my chest hitting the sheet that covered
me. That was a good thing; it helped make me snap back into
the moment. I took a long, deep breath through my nose to
smell my comfort, and it calmed me down right away. As I
felt myself fall into a slumber, I was startled by a thunderous
crash. It sounded like the house was caving in.

BANG BANG BANG. My bedroom door was vibrating
with each blow. "Get me out of this place!" a female voice
shouted. "I hate this place, I need my smoke, I need my
smoke," she yelled.

By the volume of the screams, I could tell whoever it was
had to be close to my room. I jumped out of bed to lock my
door. To my dismay, there was no lock. Panic-stricken, I put
my back against the door and slid down to the floor, knowing
my legs wouldn't hold me up; I was trembling too much. I

also knew that my 110 pound body wouldn't keep that mad sounding girl from charging into my room, but I stayed there anyway.

BANG BANG again.

"Let me out of this place before I kill someone! I need my smoke!"

I knew at that point that whoever it was must be punching her door or walls. I then heard Sister Rita's voice, and running coming from the hallway. "Stop it, Elandra, calm down!" She yelled. I put my ear up against the door to try to hear what was happening. When I heard her name, I realized it was the girl who drank my tea that afternoon.

Her screams filled the air again. "I need my smoke, I hate it here!"

Sister Rita replied with a shaky voice, "You can smoke downstairs in the smoking room."

"No, I need my smoke. My crack, man. I want to leave now; I have to get out of here."

"You can't leave now, it's almost midnight, now get back to bed."

"I need to leave," she cried.

"You have two choices. You can either go back to bed, or I call the police and they can take you out of here. I promise we will take care of this in the morning. Now, if I were you, I'd choose bed."

One more loud bang echoed through the house. It was probably from Elandra, hitting or kicking the door. And then it was quiet, with the exception of Sister's fading footsteps. I stood up and scanned the room for something to barricade my door with. There was nothing besides the dresser, which I'm sure wouldn't go over too big with the sisters. I was feeling so frightened, I turned the light on, got back into bed, slid underneath the covers, and faced the door. I wanted to be ready in case she decided to come into my room. What I was ready for, I didn't know. Not more than two minutes later, I nearly jumped out of my skin when I heard a light tapping on my door.

"It's us, Maria and Shannon," Maria whispered. "Can we come in?"

"Come on in," I whispered back with relief. With a soft squeak, the door opened. Maria and Shannon tiptoed into my room with their pillows and blankets in hand.

Shannon looked at me, pleading with her eyes and voice, "Do you mind if we sleep in here? We're scared of that new girl."

"I'd be happy, I'm frightened, too. What's wrong with her? Wait, she's new here?"

"She got here yesterday. I think she's on probation or something, that's why Sister couldn't let her leave."

Maria chimed in, "She seems pretty strange." Shannon nodded in agreement.

"She smokes crack and she's pregnant? That's so sad. What do you think they'll do with her tomorrow?" I asked.

"Maybe they'll send her to one of those detox places or something. In the meantime, we better get some sleep, some of us have to get up for school in the morning," Shannon said as she cleared her throat and pulled the blanket over her head. Neither one of the girls mentioned me turning the light off, so it stayed on all night.

"Good morning, girls."

I sat straight up. I didn't know where I was at first. Sitting on the floor were two familiar looking girls, with messy hair and blank stares on their faces. Behind them stood Sister Rita with her arms folded, and a very forbidding look on her face "Why are you girls in here?"

Maria looked up at her. "We were scared of that girl."

"She'll be leaving today. Shannon, get ready for school, and no more sleeping in each other's rooms. You girls will soon be having babies; you shouldn't be acting like babies."

I didn't have a reputation for being bold, so I surprised myself when I began to speak. "With all due respect, Sister, I hardly think I'm acting like a baby because I'm scared to sleep behind an unlocked door, when a girl with a serious problem is in the room next to me. We all heard her say she would kill someone if she couldn't leave. Isn't that reason enough for our fear? Besides, there is safety in numbers. Surely you understand, Sister." I stopped speaking and looked nervously, waiting for her response. There was none. Sister put her head down and walked out of the room. Not another word was spoken about it. She must have understood.

Shannon left for high school with the rest of the girls, except for Maria, poor Elandra, and of course, me. I was extremely grateful Maria was there with me, and would be even more grateful when Elandra wasn't.

After a breakfast of English muffins and eggs, Maria got up to clear the table. "I get stuck with kitchen duty nearly every morning, except when the other girls are off from school, which is basically just the weekends. Glad you're here to help me now."

"What do you do for the rest of the time the girls are in school?" I asked as I helped her clear the table.

"Pretty much what I want to do. Most of the volunteers here are really sweet; I hang around with them sometimes. I help them out in the office, like with filing paper work and stuff. I like helping them out. I figure they do a lot for us, ya know?"

I nodded in agreement, and then changed the subject. "What about your baby, are you keeping it?"

"I'm not sure yet. I'm considering adoption." I could tell it was hard for her to even say it.

"Me too," I added. "It's still unbelievable to me that I'm in this situation, having to make this decision. I feel like I'm living someone else's life."

At that point we had made our way into the messy kitchen. Maria turned the faucet on and began to wash the dishes, and I, with the help of Maria's directions, put the food away. "Do you have a counselor yet?" Maria asked loudly so I could hear her over the running water.

"Yeah, her name is Elizabeth, she's from Catholic Charities."

"Really? Me too. Well, I mean I go to Catholic Charities, too. My counselor's name is Sharon. Maybe they can arrange our appointments around the same time so we can go together."

"That would be great. Elizabeth is supposed to call me sometime today to check on me, you know, to see how I'm holding up here. I'll be sure to mention it to her."

"That sounds good." Maria continued washing the dishes. I grabbed a damp dish towel off the counter and began to dry them.

"So how are you holding up?" Maria asked with a smile.

"So far I'm okay. I have to tell you, I am really grateful you and Shannon are here. You're both making the transition a little easier for me, thanks for that."

"You're welcome. I have a feeling we're going to be good friends."

"I do too, Maria."

That morning was the first of many times Maria and I would clean the kitchen together and occasionally share very deep conversations. It was also the start of a cherished and memorable friendship.

Dinner was awkward that night. Elandra was still there. Apparently, they were waiting for a bed in a nearby rehab center. I sat through the whole meal trying to figure out a way to sneak a chair upstairs to barricade my door with, in case Elandra didn't get her spot in rehab before bedtime. Both scenarios were looking rather grim, unfortunately.

"I got an 86 on my English quiz today," Pat blurted out.

Pat was a pretty girl. She had a flawless complexion and blonde curly hair. She was 16 years old, but looked more like 12. She was fairly quiet, and at that point in time I didn't know if it was shyness or indifference. I later found out it was a little bit of both.

"Should we clap our hands now, or later?" Debbie asked with a smirk as she picked up her glass of milk and took a sip. Debbie was 17 years old. There was nothing about her appearance that stood out. I guess I would describe her as pretty. She had fair skin, with small dark eyes and black wavy hair. She had an extremely tough exterior, which I saw right through. We would later become considerably friendly with each other.

"Shut up, Debbie!" Pat shouted with a defeated look on her face. Pat and Debbie's little tiffs were not infrequent.. Looking back, I realized Debbie needed to have something over on someone in that house. Pat was the perfect target, and after all, she fed into it. Being that I was one of the oldest girls there, I tried to be the mature one and help keep the peace. I often spoke to Debbie about her childish behavior. Her tormenting never really stopped, but they became more infrequent. I explained to Pat that it was basically a game to Debbie. She lived with it until she left, which was four months later, after giving birth to a pretty little girl. That ends the story of Pat and Debbie.

"That is enough bickering girls, now finish your dinner and then go upstairs and finish your homework," Sister Rita said sternly.

Maria glanced at me, "Guess we're on kitchen duty again." She took her eyes off of me and onto the four women who just walked into the dining room. Two of them appeared to be in their mid to late twenties, while the other two looked to be about forty. All of them had short hair, and were dressed neatly in skirts and blouses.

"Oh, hi, Sisters," Maria said.

"Who are these young ladies?" one of the younger sisters asked in a delicate voice.

"I'm Jane, and this is Elandra." I stood up to shake their hands. Elandra just sat there stone faced, poor thing. All of them politely introduced themselves to us, one at a time. Sisters Anne and Patty were the youngest of the four, the others were Sister Bridgette and Sister Noreen. All four of them worked outside Rachel Residence, and each of them had different occupations. Basically, the convent was a place for them to have their meals and lay their heads at night. Each one of them would soon become very dear to me. I guess you could call them my friends; as a matter of fact, I know you could call them my friends.

Chapter Six

Christmas Morning

The snowflakes were quickly falling; some were the size of sugar cubes. *The flakes are so big it won't stick,* I thought as I lay in my bed imagining Christmas as a child.

Me, and each of my eight siblings all stood on the landing at the top of the stairs. Sleep was still in our eyes. The older ones were grumbling, not ready to be awake. Yet, their hearts were still pounding with great anticipation of what was yet to come. Dad's voice carried up the stairs, "Okay, kids, you can come down now."

Practically falling on top of each other as we ran downstairs and into the living room, we were eager to get to where our fantasy world awaited us. The lights on the imperfect yet beautiful tree were illuminating. Ornaments hung intermittently from its branches. Some of them were newer and shiny, while others were more like antiques. They were the ones I liked best. Each one had a memory, told its own story. There was an angel ornament with a cracked wing and chipped paint. Tess and I would fight over who would hang it on the tree. We both felt sorry for it, as if it were alive. I guess in a way it was.

Tinsel shimmered from the lights. Dad insisted each strand be put on individually. "No clumping the tinsel," he would say. It made for a stunning tree. The gifts, wrapped perfectly, lay in mounds underneath it.

All of us gazed in amazement as we each took a place on the floor. The sharpest of my senses was my sense of smell. That early morning the scents of evergreen, coffee, and stale cigar left over from my Uncle Eddie the night before filled the air. Although the combination might sound repulsive, none of us minded. After all, it meant it was Christmas. My dad sat on the couch with his gray, tasseled hair wearing his burgundy paisley bathrobe, while mom sat on her piano bench facing all of us. She wore her robe as well, along with her beautiful smile, which had a hint of worry in it. She was worried one of us may be disappointed.

"Oldest first," Dad stated as he slid a package over to Grace. "For you, Grace."

The tag was written in black magic marker, and read, "To Grace, Love Santa". It took many years for me to figure out that the handwriting on all of the packages from Santa was actually my mom's. Grace began to carefully open the package in front of her. She sighed with delight as she held up a fluffy blue bathrobe.

"I love it, it's so soft." She stood up and puts it on over her pajamas, modeling it for us.

"It looks great on you, honey," Mom said with relief. I observed the exchange of expressions between my mom and Grace. There was a clear sadness in my mom's eyes. That would be the last Christmas Grace would be home with us, she was getting married a month later. Even though I was touched by the moment, I couldn't get over the fact that Grace was so excited about getting a bathrobe. Then again, I was only eight and was hoping to find a Barbie Doll under the tree.

I was brought back into the moment by the sound of tapping on my door.

"Are you awake yet, Jane? It's Christmas."

"Yeah, I'm awake. Come on in, Shannon."

Shannon burst into my room, beaming. "Come on, come on, you gotta get up. Let's go downstairs, Maria is already down there."

"What's the rush?" I asked, with little eagerness.

"What's the rush? It's Christmas morning! C'mon, get up!" she giggled as she nudged me.

"Okay, okay. I'll be right down. I need to wash up and brush my teeth. I'll meet you downstairs."

I got out of bed, grabbed my toiletry bag and headed for the bathroom. As I walked past the staircase, I could hear the song "Silent Night" coming from downstairs, along with a faint chatter from the girls. My heart sank at the sounds. I wanted to go home or back to bed, one or the other. After washing up, I walked downstairs. "Silent Night" was over, and now "I'll Be Home for Christmas" was playing. As I entered the living room I was overwhelmed by the serenity, especially because the room was filled with everyone who resided there. Except for Bing Crosby's voice singing softly in the background, the room was silent. The lights on the tree were illuminating, nearly identical ornaments from my childhood hung from it. It even had tinsel draped delicately over its branches, and mounds of presents lay beneath it. Not my mom, but nuns sat with the same look of enthusiasm and worry on their faces. I joined the rest of the moms to be, who sat on the floor around the tree.

"The oldest girl should open first," Sister Noreen announced.

"That would be me," I proudly admitted.

"For Jane." Sister Noreen slid a gift toward me. It was a box wrapped in red scotch plaid paper, wearing a big green bow, and its tag read, "For Jane, Love Rachel mothers and others."

I carefully opened the package and held up a pink bathrobe. I immediately put it on in excitement. "Oh, thank you so much."

I once again flashed back to the last Christmas Grace ever spent at our family's home. I then understood the magnitude of the giving, and understood how hard my mom and dad worked to buy all of those gifts for us. Grace appreciated receiving the bathrobe that year because she understood then what I had come to understand. I was feeling the same gratitude that very moment. All of the girls received robes that morning, and we later lined the staircase, wearing them and our bellies proudly as the sisters snapped away with their cameras. It was a Christmas I would never forget.

ॐ∞

"Hurry, Jane, the bus is going to be here in ten minutes."

"I'm coming, Maria," I shouted, while I frantically searched through my closet for a pair of gloves. "Ah ha, here they are." Quickly I squirmed into my coat, which I could barely button. I slipped my gloves on and ran down the stairs. As Maria and I stepped outside, I could feel the cold cut right through me.

"I didn't think it was going to be this cold out," Maria chattered through her teeth.

"I know, I should have worn a hat."

We began to run against what felt like an arctic wind down an alley that led to Rose Street to catch the bus. I could feel my face beginning to numb as I ran. Tears from the cold wind formed lines of water across my temples.

"Just in time," Maria said as the dirty bus came to a screeching halt in front of us. We climbed the steps into the bus to find about 20 pairs of eyes staring us up and down, something all of us girls began to get used to. I wiped the tears off of my face and slid into the last available seat alongside Maria. My strong sense of smell kicked in immediately. I covered my nose with my gloved hand to keep myself from vomiting. "Ooh, somebody must have gotten sick on this bus" gagged Maria.

"No kidding," I mumbled. As I looked around the bus I noticed no one else seemed affected by it. I guess it was because we were pregnant that it was more noticeable. Maria and I sat with our noses covered the rest of the trip downtown.

As we turned onto Franklin Street, I reached up to pull the cord, signaling the bus driver to stop. He abruptly pulled over, stopped the bus and opened the door. Both Maria and I stepped out, welcoming the cold fresh air that hit our faces. We walked toward the building that read "Catholic Charities," the same building I first went to with Shana, and the same one I went to four additional times with Maria. We walked through the familiar "Adoption Services" door and approached the same receptionist that had worked there five months before. "Hey girls, how are you feeling?" she asked us, smiling broadly..

"We're okay, how are you?" Maria responded.

"I'm just fine. I'll tell Sharon and Elizabeth that you're here."

"Thanks," I said softly, looking at her with a hint of jealousy. I couldn't help it. She was about my age, thin, attractive, and not pregnant. She was also a true reminder of what a mess I made of my life.

She put down the telephone receiver and looked up at us.

"They're both ready for the two of you. Go on ahead in to their offices."

Elizabeth was sitting behind her desk when I arrived at her doorway. "Hi, honey, come on in and have a seat." I walked my now awkward and very pregnant body into her office and plopped down in the chair opposite Elizabeth.

"I think I found the perfect couple to adopt your baby." My heart sank. "My baby." Those words and the reality of them, it was such a surreal moment for me.

"Oh?" I questioned sadly.

"Yes, they applied for adoption several years ago. Twice they were told they would be receiving a child, and both times the birth mother changed her mind the last minute."

"Oh, that's so sad. They must have been devastated."

"They were heartbroken, but they were aware ahead of time that situations such as the mother changing her mind could occur. I'm sure even though they knew it could happen; it was hard to be fully prepared. Anyway, they are very good people, and are waiting for the day they can bring a baby home."

"Can you tell me about them?"

"Well, I can tell you some things about them. The potential adoptive mother is described as a very warm, loving person. She's a special education teacher, apparently quite dedicated to her students. She actually has some of them spend occasional weekends with her."

"Wow. That takes a special person. How does her husband feel about that?"

"From what I hear, they both love having the children."

"They sound really nice. What does he do for a living?"

"He's a lawyer."

"Are they Catholic? It's very important to me that this baby is raised Catholic."

"Yes, they are practicing Catholics."

"They do sound like good people, but how do I know that they're good enough?"

Elizabeth looked at me with a great deal of sympathy. "Honey, I can tell you that all of the couples who apply for adoption are screened beyond screened. I can also tell you that I've met this couple. I can honestly say I consider myself a good judge of character. I think they are a lovely couple, who unfortunately were unable to give birth to their own child. They will be loving parents, if not to your child to another child." Elizabeth paused for a brief moment. "Think about it for a while. Let me know when you can."

"No, no. I don't need to think about it. They are the right couple, my heart is telling me to pick them. I want them to adopt my baby." As hard as those words were to say, I knew it was right. I felt a great deal of sadness, yet a true sense of peace. My decision was made and I knew from the core of my being that it was the right choice — they were the right choice.

Chapter Seven

A Midnight in Spring

Oh boy. My eyes popped open. I could feel pain surging through me, radiating from my lower back around to my stomach. My belly tightened with the pain until it was hard as rock. Man, this hurts, I thought, as I remembered my doctor's words. "If you can't sleep through the cramping, it's probably labor." Slowly my belly began to soften, and the pain began to ease. I looked at the clock, it said 12:07. No sooner did I close my eyes than the wrenching pain returned. This time, the clock said 12:18. My heart began to race. I knew I was probably in labor. I closed my eyes one more time; only eight minutes had passed since the last one.

When the third contraction subsided, I took the opportunity to walk to the bathroom, with hopes of my walk being pain free. I turned the bathroom light on to find that I was bleeding. The room began to spin. I managed to find the nearest wall, and slowly lowered myself down to the floor. I need to calm down, women do this every day. I then thankfully recalled my mother's words. "I was never really afraid of labor, I just prayed through each one," she would say. My mother did everything gracefully. I couldn't help but think of how much I wanted her there at that moment. I was a little afraid, and was not looking forward to the next contraction.

Grace, I thought, I need to call Grace.

I sat on the bathroom floor through two more fairly strong contractions. I finally got up and walked to Sister Rita's bedroom.

"Sister Rita." I tapped lightly on her door. "Sister Rita, it's me, Jane. I think it's time," I whispered. A few seconds passed before the door opened. Sister stood there with tasseled hair, eyes half closed, and without her glasses. I hardly recognized her. She looked so different without them. She looked younger and not like a nun.

"How far apart are your contractions?" she asked, with

raspy sound to her voice. I responded in a bit of a panic.

"Well, they aren't exactly consistent, maybe eight to ten minutes apart, but I'm bleeding and the contractions won't let me sleep."

"Okay. Wait a little while, maybe take a shower, then come back and get me if they continue. She gave me a little smirk and shut the door.

Feeling a bit defeated, I made my way back to my room to gather my toiletries and some clean comfortable clothes, and sat down on my bed waiting for the next contraction. I knew I was in labor. Mustering up the strength, I traipsed back to the bathroom, got undressed as quickly as I could and stepped into the shower, letting the warm water run over my tightened belly, which was once again contracting. As I looked down I came to the realization that this was the last day my baby would be inside of me. I waited nine months for that day. It was here, and I wasn't as happy about it as I thought I would be. I would miss the feeling of carrying a life inside of me. I'd even miss the baby's kicks and hiccups. My heart began to ache with the thought as once again a stabbing pain crawled from my lower back to my stomach. This pain had come much quicker than the last, and felt much more intense. I leaned up against the shower wall until it subsided, then quickly got out, dried off, and got dressed before the next contraction had a chance to attack me.

I immediately went to Sister Rita's room and knocked again. This time when the door opened, Sister was fully dressed. Her glasses were on and her hair was combed. I must have had a painful look on my face when I expressed, "This has to be it!"

Sister looked back at me. "Yes, I can tell. I'll go ahead and call Grace for you. I'll tell her to meet us at the hospital. Leave your suitcase at the top of the stairs. I'll carry it down for you. Just go downstairs and sit on the couch, I'll be right there." After retrieving my suitcase (I already had it packed), I dropped it at the top of the stairs and proceeded to go down to the living room to wait for Sister. A few minutes later she arrived in the living room with my bag and her umbrella in hand. "Are you ready, Jane?"

"I am as ready as I'll ever be," I said sarcastically.

We were about to step outside when I heard the girls' voices coming from the top of the stairs "Good luck, Jane!" Debbie shouted as the rest of the girls chimed in with their wish-you-wells. One at a time they walked downstairs half asleep, each taking turns hugging me. Maria and Shannon were the last to say goodbye. We instinctively group hugged. "You'll be fine, it'll be cake," Maria joked.

Shannon chimed in, "I don't want to hear any horror stories about labor."

Maria elbowed Shannon, "Don't scare her."

"It's okay, I'll be fine. I'll call you when it's all over."

Sister Rita and I stepped out into the dark rainy night, the leaves on the trees whistled above us as we passed them. Into the car we went to begin our 30-minute journey to the hospital. It seemed longer than a half an hour, with my having many pains along the way. As we approached the E.R., the rain was coming down in buckets. The sounds of sirens echoed around us.

"I'll drop you off at the door and meet you inside, just wait in the corridor for me."

"Okay," I said as Sister pulled up to the E.R doors.

I stepped into the rain. Within seconds a security guard stood in front of me with a wheelchair. "Chauffer at your service," he said with a huge grin.

"Oh, thank you," I said while holding my belly and lowering myself into the chair.

"Let me guess. Maternity?"

"That would be a yes," I moaned.

Sister Rita ran up beside us. "Wait for me!"

Wheeling me to the maternity ward, the very pleasant gentleman whistled to the tune of "Tiny Bubbles." If I wasn't so uncomfortable, I probably would have enjoyed the entertainment. He slowly brought the wheelchair to a stop in front of a set of double doors marked "Maternity and Delivery".

"This would be your stop." He pressed a large button to the right of the doors. Both doors swung open inward. He proceeded to wheel me in and stopped at the first desk he came to. "Delivery for a delivery!" he said.

Man, is this guy always this pleasant? I glanced over at the nurse sitting behind the desk. I knew by the look on her face she wasn't going to be anywhere near as pleasant as the security guard.

"Well, best wishes to you, young lady."

My attention turned from the tough-looking nurse to Mr. Pleasant. "Oh, thank you for the ride and for being so nice to me." He tipped his hat, smiled, and walked through the double doors, finishing his rendition of "Tiny Bubbles."

Just then, the nurse behind the desk stood up, all six feet of her. "I'm Helga, what's your story?"

"Hi Helga, this is Jane," Sister Rita said, sounding as intimidated as I felt. Helga walked around the desk and began to wheel me into the labor room.

"What's your story?" she asked, still sounding agitated.

"Well, I'm having pains every few minutes."

"Few? What's a few?"

I wanted to give the right answer, but I knew I wouldn't be. "Every eight minutes or so."

"You're here too soon."

Sister Rita began to put her two cents in, "Well, I really feel it's best if she's here. Not only has she had consistent contractions, but she's bleeding as well. On top of that, she's two weeks over due."

Helga glanced over at me and grabbed one of those silly gowns at the same time. "I suppose you should stay. We'll have the attending doctor examine you. In the meantime, put this gown on with the opening in the back. I'll go ahead and page the doctor."

"Will you be okay if I run to the vending machine for a cup of coffee?" Sister asked.

"Sure, I'm fine, go ahead."

I slowly walked to the bathroom that was adjacent to the labor room. Another pain ripped through me. I gasped and grabbed the handle on the wall and held onto it until the pain subsided. I then changed into the gown. Unable to tie it myself, I held it closed with one hand and held my clothes in the other. I shuffled out of the bathroom over to the bed. I dropped my clothes on a nearby chair and began to slide myself on the bed. That's when I noticed Grace and Sister standing in the doorway, both with a great deal of sympathy written all over their faces.

"Are you okay?" Grace walked towards me with her arms outstretched. "It's going to be okay." In all honesty a hug was not what I was in the mood for, but I accepted Grace's embrace. After all, it wasn't her fault I was in this situation. "Why don't you lie down, Jane?" She helped me swing my legs around and onto the bed.

"Oh, no, here comes another one," I cried.

"Breathe Jane, breathe, in through the nose, out through the mouth," Grace gently demanded as she took hold of my hand. I lay there with my eyes closed, relishing the pain-free moments, knowing the next contraction would inevitably be coming sooner than the last and would probably be more painful.

Grace looked at Sister. "How far apart are her contractions now?"

"Oh, I'd say every five minutes or so. Is that about right, Jane?" Keeping my eyes closed, I shook my head in agreement.

"Hey, you may go as fast as Kathy and I did."

"How fast is that?" Sister asked.

"Well," Grace responded, "I had all four of my children in less than five hours. My sister Kathy had her daughter Erin 15 minutes after she arrived at the hospital."

"Wow Jane, maybe you'll be as lucky as your sisters."

At that moment, I looked at the clock. It was 3:45 a.m. I would have to have the baby in the next hour and a half in order to compete with Grace. Beating Kathy's record was obviously out of the question. The rest of the morning dragged on with not much change, my contractions stayed pretty much the same for hours. Grace was a great support, feeding me ice chips, rubbing my lower back, and doing the Lamaze breathing with me, which I needed to do, because I refused to take any pain medication. Grace was also great at having the doctor examine me every hour, which was both excruciating and frustrating. At 1 p.m. I was still only two centimeters dilated. Finally, at about 2 p.m., when the doctor came to examine me again he said, "I think it's time to break your water, but first the nurses are going to bring you into the birthing room. It's available for you to use. I think you'll be more comfortable in there."

Before I had another contraction, two nurses came in and wheeled me into the birthing room. It was a fairly nice room. The curtains were open, which helped send a significant amount of light in. The bed didn't look like a hospital bed; it looked like a bed you would find in a nice hotel. End tables sat on either side of the bed, each had pastel blue lamps on them. The room even had a television and a carpet, to boot. No sooner did the nurses get me into bed than the doctor walked in with what looked like a crochet hook in his hand.

"Oh no, what is that?"

"I know it looks scary, but trust me, you won't even feel it," he said. I immediately looked over at Grace. She shook her head yes while giving me a reassuring look, and then she took hold of my hand again. They were both right; I didn't feel a thing, just a gush of water.

"There, that should move things along for you. I'll be back in ten minutes to check you again."

The next three contractions felt ten times more intense. I didn't know how much more I could take without having any medication to at least ease the agony a little. The doctor came in 15 minutes later and examined me with gloved hands.

"Well, Jane, you are four centimeters now and 90% effaced. I have to go to my office now. I'll come back this evening to see you. I'm sure you'll have your baby before tomorrow. You're progressing nicely."

"Before tomorrow? Progressing nicely? I want this baby out now!" I cried.

"I'm sure you do, but that's not the way it works. The baby will come when the baby is ready." He was so condescending. I thought if I had a woman doctor, she wouldn't have spoken to me that way after being in hours of pain. Then I remembered Helga. I guess gender has nothing to do with one's rudeness, it's the person.

Within minutes of my male pal leaving, I was lying on my side, rocking back and forth literally pulling at my bangs from their roots. I was in such harrowing pain I wouldn't let Grace near me, never mind touch me. I knew she felt awful, that she wanted to help me. I was beyond help at that point. I couldn't talk, I didn't want ice chips, and I definitely didn't want my back rubbed. It took all I had to stop myself from screaming. I can recall Grace seeming anxious in those moments. She began rummaging through her purse. She pulled out a lollypop, probably given to her by a bank teller for little Barbara. It seemed to me that she was pretty happy to find it. She opened the clear wrapper and started to eat it. I could smell the pungent scent of grapes.

"I feel like I'm going to get sick, get that lollypop away from me!"

"Are you nauseous?" Grace asked with a twinge of panic mixed with a little too much enthusiasm.

"You must be in transition, I'll get a nurse." She didn't return with a nurse, but with a female P.A., who she practically dragged into the room. "You have to check her, she said she was nauseous. I think she's in transition."

Looking both startled and a bit annoyed, the P.A. replied, "She can't be, Dr Jacobs filled me in before he left the floor and said she was only four centimeters."

"Trust me," Grace replied; "if she's anything like me or my sister, she'll go from four to ten in no time, please just trust me and check her," Grace pleaded.

"Okay," she said reluctantly, "I'll check her." She reached into her pocket and pulled out a rubber glove. While checking me she had a shocked look on her face. "Wow, you are nine and a half centimeters." With a fearful expression, she ran to the door, "Page Dr Jacobs, stat, we have a baby coming, now!" she shouted.

Helga ran into the room. "Dr Jacobs is already at his office, he just called here," she said to the P.A. "you'll have to deliver the baby." Then she looked at Grace. "If you want to be in here for the delivery you need to put some greens on. Go to the nurses' station, and ask one of the aides to give some to you."

Grace looked at me with pleading eyes. "Please don't have this baby before I get back."

"I'll try not to, Grace," I groaned loudly.

At that point everything seemed to be going in fast motion. Before I knew it there were about five or six people in the room. One of the staff wheeled in a tiny crib that appeared to be made out of glass or a hard plastic. I remember thinking, wow, that's for my baby.

"Put your legs in the stirrups, honey, and slide down to the end of the table, best you can, and whatever you do dear, don't push," Helga said politely, which shocked me. With an incredible amount of effort, I did what I was asked, my entire body trembling in the process.

"Good girl," the P. A. said, "you're doing just fine." I began to breathe the way I was taught in Lamaze class, in order to not push the baby out. Apparently, I was doing it a little too fast. I could feel my mouth starting to go numb and beads of sweat forming on my forehead. Feeling the blood leaving my face, the room spun out of control.

I heard myself ever so faintly say, "I'm going to pass out, I'm going to pass out."

"She's hyperventilating, get a paper bag!" the P.A. shouted.

Within seconds, a masked lady wearing blue scrubs placed a brown paper bag over my nose and mouth. "It's okay, honey, breathe slowly, you're almost done." Almost immediately I began to feel the blood come back into my face, then the numbness disappeared. I started to feel way more than I wanted to. I experienced pressure and pain like I never had before; a loud involuntary scream accompanied it. Out of the corner of my eye I saw Grace run back in. She came right over and stood to the side of me where I could see her.

In that moment I felt an incredible urge to push, while again, forced screeching came from the core of my being and out of my mouth. I had no control over it. "You can push with this one Jane, push with all you have," The P.A. said as she sat at the bottom of my feet. I did, and when I did, it surprisingly lessened the pain.

"You're doing great, Jane," Grace said as she patted the sweat off my forehead with a tissue. I looked up at her and saw only her eyes, as her face was covered in a surgical mask. She looked back at me with a great amount of empathy.

Another short minute passed before another fierce pain tore through me again.

"Push, Jane, bear down!" Helga shouted.

"Oh God, I can't do this!" I screamed. I pushed with every ounce of energy I thought I had left.

"Head's out," the P.A said calmly. There was silence in the room and a bit of tension in the air. "Stop pushing Jane, I'll let you know when you can push again."

"Oh God, here comes another one!" I shouted.

Grace squeezed my hand. "Blow out with this one, Jane"

It was clear to me that she knew what was happening, but I was clueless. All that I knew was that I wanted it to be over.

"Go ahead, Jane, you can push," the P.A. said. I bore down with all my exhausted body could manage, while letting out a blood-curdling scream at the same time.

"It's a girl!" the P.A. exclaimed with relief. Silence filled the room again, then a sweet cry.

I looked at Grace once again, only seeing her pretty green eyes. Tears fell from them. "She is so beautiful, she is perfect," she said. I couldn't cry. I felt no emotion in that moment, just relief that the pain was over. The P.A. lifted my little girl up to show her to me, then handed her over to a nurse who wrapped her in a blanket and whisked her away. I thought it was odd that she wasn't placed in the crib that was bought in earlier. The nurse had carried her out.

Rather confused, I asked Grace, "Why did they take her away, is everything okay, is she okay?" I started to get a little panicky.

Grace, still overcome with emotion, said, "She is just fine. They need to check her out in the nursery. Your umbilical cord was wrapped around her neck, but she was breathing fine. I'm sure they're doing it for precautionary reasons." Grace seemed fairly calm about it so, in turn, my panic slowly began to disappear.

Chapter Eight

Two hours later

"When will they let me see her?" I asked, rather impatiently. I was so exhausted, and needed to see her to confirm in my mind and heart what had happened only couple of hours before.

"I'm sure as soon as they finish examining her. It's a process, you know."

Looking at Grace, I knew she was as eager as I was, and she looked to be just as exhausted. Her arms were folded and her head was down as she paced the floor back and forth. Every once in a while she would glance up at the clock on the wall, attempting to do so inconspicuously. I'm sure she was trying to not make me more anxious than I already was.

"You did such a good job today, Jane, I'm so very proud of you. You were a real trooper having had no meds. It wasn't such a short labor either," she said as she walked over and sat at the end of my bed.

"Thanks Grace," I said, "you know...for being my coach today, and being there for me all along."

"I wouldn't have wanted to be anywhere else," she said, grinning and fluttering her eyes, something Grace had a habit of doing, especially when she was extremely serious about a point she was trying to make. I smiled back, then we just sat, both of us not really being able to muster up another word or ounce of emotion. It was strange. Grace and I were never at a loss for words, we were just completely wiped out in every way.

Just then an unfamiliar nurse wheeled in a tiny crib with a pink index card taped to it. It read, "BABY ROSS, 6LBS, 13OZ. 20 IN. LONG."

"Baby Ross," she announced, then left the crib and left the room. Inside the crib lay a tiny infant. All that was exposed was her head, the rest of her wrapped tightly in a white receiving blanket. She was fast asleep.

Instinctively I began to get up. "Stay put, I'll bring her to you." Grace walked over to the crib, scooped her up and cradled her in the nook of her arm. "Oh my goodness, she is so beautiful."

"Can I hold her now, Grace?"

Grace began to cry. She lifted my baby up to her face and kissed her on the cheek, no sounds came from the baby. She was still in a sound sleep.

"Please don't cry Grace, at least not yet, we need to enjoy this time with her." At that point I was clueless as to what pain we would go through in the next few days. Grace was crying because she knew; after all, she was a mother herself. Grace looked up at me. I could tell she felt guilty for crying, then I felt guilty for saying that to her.

"Can I hold her now?" I asked, knowing I looked very eager.

"Oh, I'm so sorry." Grace walked over to me and placed the baby in my arms. Surreal is the only way to describe how I felt.

Grace stayed with me for some time. We took turns holding the baby. It was inevitable that she had to go home to be with her own family. I didn't want her to go, now feeling more bonded with her than I had my whole life, which I didn't think was possible. She promised she would be back, kissed us both, and left reluctantly.

The next few hours went by rather quickly. To me, it felt like no time at all. I spent those hours staring at my precious daughter, examining every inch of her. I started at her head, stroking her soft dirty blonde hair (the little there was of it). Her eyes were shut, very far set and long. I guessed that meant she would have big eyes. Her nose was small, she had pink cheeks, and rosebud lips…she really was pretty. I unwrapped her from her blanket to expose her tiny little body. Her legs were so skinny and pulled up close to her belly. I counted her toes, there we five on each foot. I was amazed at how tiny her toenails were. I slipped her fragile hands out of the mitts of her undershirt. As I stroked her soft skin as I counted five fingers on each one. She was perfect, a true miracle. I changed her, fed her (though she didn't eat much), then I stared some more.

Even though I didn't want to, I eventually I decided to lay her down in her crib. It was hard, but I knew it was best; I needed to sleep. The clock read 10:00 p.m., which meant it had been nearly 24 hours since my labor had begun, and I hadn't slept at all since then.

Just as I began to doze off, a nurse walked into my room, one I hadn't seen before. "There is someone downstairs that says she is your sister from out of town." She said it with the voice of a child that matched her baby face and small frame.

"My sister?" I asked with surprise. I couldn't imagine who it could be. After all, Grace had just left, and Kathy, Tess and Chrissie lived 600 miles away.

"Yeah. Normally we would not allow her to come up, but since she has traveled so far we'll give her a few minutes to visit."

"Oh, thank you." I sat up in the bed and waited with great anticipation, excited about seeing any one of my sisters. A few moments later, a slender petite dark-haired girl walked into my room. Though that could have described any of my sisters, there was absolutely no mistaking it was Shana

"Hey kiddo," she said as she placed a basket of tulips on my night stand.

"Shana, what are you doing here? How did you find out I had the baby?"

"I happened to be home for a wedding. I called Elizabeth to see what was happening with you. I was pleasantly surprised to hear you had the baby today; and a girl… Congrats! You won't believe this Jane, but I had my little girl three years ago today! How unbelievable is that?"

I'm sure I had a look of shock on my face, but the truth is, inside I wasn't surprised at all. Everything that had happened to me up to that point, most would say was coincidental, but I would say they were miracles.

"That is really amazing,"

We both looked at each other smiling. Nothing needed to be said, as we both knew what the other was feeling. Both of us were filled with sadness, but wearing smiles. I broke the silence

"How is school going?"

"It's going okay. Some of the classes are kind of difficult, but I'm enjoying it. I plan on being there for awhile; it's going to take some time to get my Master's."

"It'll be worth it Shana, you'll make an amazing special ed. teacher. You always had such a great way with Billy and those guys!"

"Well, they were the best." Shana walked over to the crib to take a peek at the baby, who was still asleep. "She's beautiful, Jane," Shana said as she laid her hand on the baby's back. She looked at me and smiled, "You will get through this, and remember, I'm always here for you."

I replied with little emotion, "I know."

It was as if I was in denial of what was yet to happen, but Shana knew. Just then the little nurse peeked into the room. She let us know it was time for Shana to go. Shana walked over to me and gave me a hug. "Call me if you need to talk, you hear me, kiddo?"

"Sure, Shana. Thanks so much for taking the time to come up and see me, and for all you have done for me, I'll never forget it."

She smiled her beautiful smile, blew me a kiss and walked out the door, surely filled with much emotion, for what she had been through three years prior on that very day.

Morning arrived quickly. As soon as I woke, I sat up and realized where I was. I looked over towards the crib, and it wasn't there. Panic soared through me. I leaned over to press the button to call the nurse's station. "Yes?" shrieked a woman's voice from the wall behind me. "Can I help you?"

"My baby, where's my baby? Someone took my baby!"

"Relax doll, your baby is in the nursery, we brought her down last night, you needed your sleep."

"Oh, okay. Can I have her back?" I replied with a great deal of relief.

"Someone will bring her down to you in a few minutes."

Those few minutes gave me the time to shuffle to the bathroom to change. It took some time because the episiotomy was extremely painful. They gave me Tucks to relieve the pain, which helped a little, very little, (I can still smell the scent of the witch hazel that they were soaked in). I changed my gown, washed my face, brushed my teeth, combed my hair, and walked slowly back to bed. Two minutes later a young girl dressed in a pink and white striped dress wheeled a crib into my room. "Here she is" she announced. She took the baby out of the crib. With a big smile she placed her in my arms. "She just had a bottle. She'll need to be burped though."

"Okay, thanks," I said, grateful for her kindness. I got the feeling the whole ward knew I was giving her up for adoption, but no one was very kind to me. I felt like they were all judging me. Then again, maybe it was just me judging myself. She left the room with a wave. I placed the baby over my shoulder, tapping her back ever so gently. After a few moments I heard the sound of a faint burp. I took her off my shoulder and placed her in the nook of my arm to look at her precious face again. That's when I noticed that she had spit up.

I wiggled myself off the bed and reached into the bottom of the crib where there were fresh undershirts and diapers. I grabbed an undershirt. Laying the baby on the bed I leaned over to change her. I removed her soiled shirt and put it by my pillow. I decided then that I wasn't leaving the hospital without it. Dirty or not, she had worn it, and I needed to take something of hers with me. I would stick it in my overnight bag. I got back into bed. I gazed at my little girl once again in amazement at the tiny, perfect, precious miracle. Awake, she stared back at me with big dark eyes. My heart ached with the thought of parting from her.

After accidently dozing off again, I awoke to a cold hand shaking my arm. "Jane, it's me, Elizabeth. Let me take the baby. Thank heaven you didn't drop her, falling asleep with her in your arms like that." She took the baby out of my arms and laid her on her belly in the crib. "I know this is going to be difficult for you, but you have to sign the adoption papers today."

My heart sank. "Grace will be here in a bit. Can we wait until she gets here?"

Grace walked in right at that moment.

"Perfect timing," Elizabeth said, a bit too cheerfully considering the sadness Grace and I were feeling. Surely, she must have known that. I was shocked at how insensitive she was being. I was actually taken off guard by her attitude. It now felt like it was a business transaction. Maybe I was being overly sensitive, but circumstances being what they were, I guess I expected a little more compassion.

Grace walked over to the baby, leaned over and gave her a kiss, then over to me and did the same thing. "Elizabeth, can I talk to my sister in private for a moment, please?"

Elizabeth smiled at Grace. "Sure, no problem, I'll wait out in the hallway."

I looked at Grace in confusion. "What's up?"

"Well, Jane, Tim and I were talking. We both want you to know that we'll support you in whatever decision you make. What I mean is, you don't have to sign those papers if you aren't ready. You don't have to sign them at all if you don't want to."

I looked at her in disbelief. "What? What do you mean? I can't take care of her. I don't have a job, a place to live. Besides, how could I ever do that to the couple that's expecting her? It wouldn't be right. No, she belongs to them. As much as I hate to admit it, I feel it in my heart. I don't want to feel it, but I do. She belongs to that couple; they are who she is supposed to be with."

Grace looked at me half-smiling and crying at the same time. "I feel the same way, but I needed to hear it from you. I couldn't let you sign those papers unless I knew you were sure. I said that to you for your sake and the sake of your little angel. I love you both, you understand?"

"Sure, I understand, and I appreciate why you said it," I whispered sadly. "Can you get Elizabeth in here now? I want to get this over with."

Grace nodded, grabbed a tissue off my night stand, wiped her eyes, and left to get Elizabeth. I proceeded to look over the papers as Elizabeth described to me in layman's terms what each line meant. I finally got to the last page, and had to sign. It was a bunch of legal jargon: I (dotted line) hereby surrender Baby (dotted line) to (dotted line) on such and such day, et cetera.

I signed on the dotted line and literally felt like I was signing my life away, knowing signing my life away was what

I was supposed to do — I knew it in my heart. Elizabeth left shortly after I signed the papers. Grace stayed for a while. We mostly sat in silence feeling defeated until my friends from Rachel Residence walked in, including, of course, my faithful friends Maria and Shannon. Each took turns holding the baby, giggling and smiling, except for poor Maria who wore a half smile-while her eyes filled with tears. After all, she was due one week from then and planned to give her child up for adoption, too. It was early evening by the time everyone left. I was glad to see them come, I was glad to see them go. Although I never wanted Grace to leave, it was nice to have some alone time with my baby.

Eventually I put her in her crib and lay on my side staring at over at her. I think I'll name her Mary Grace, I thought, yes, Mary Grace.

Chapter Nine

I could feel the warmth of the sun on my face, my eyes still unopened. I delighted in the sound of the chirping birds. I slowly opened my eyes to find an Asian woman lying in the bed opposite me. Balloons stating, "It's a boy" floated above her bed. As I gazed at her I was quickly reminded of where I was, and the dreadful day that awaited me.

I'm ashamed to say I envied the new mother lying there. She was bringing her baby home, and I wasn't. Once again I felt my eyes pooling up with water, which in mere seconds turned to flooding tears. Sobbing for what seemed like the one hundredth time in two days, I wondered how I had any tears left to cry. With my heart pounding I sat up and wiped my swollen eyes. I turned to look at Mary Grace to find her missing once again. Obviously, a nurse must have taken her back to the nursery during the night. I glanced over at the clock on the wall. 6:00 a.m. I remembered Elizabeth saying she would be arriving around 10:00, which gave me four more hours with Mary. I found my way to the bathroom, still feeling a lot of pain from the episiotomy. As quickly as I could I washed up and fixed my hair, and even put a drop of my makeup on. I knew Mary Grace wouldn't remember me, but I still wanted to look nice in the last few hours we would spend together.

Between my eagerness to see Mary Grace and the pain I was feeling from my stitches, the corridor leading to the nursery seemed especially long that morning. Approaching the nursery, I saw a nurse inside, and I began to tap on the window. After getting her attention I pointed to Mary Grace's crib. She nodded and proceeded to wheel Mary out to me. Avoiding eye contact with her, I mumbled, "Thank you," and wheeled Mary Grace back to my room. When I walked back into my room I was relieved to find my roommate was still sleeping. I had to have this quiet time with the baby with no one watching or hearing me. As I lifted her out of the crib I took notice once again of her very long fingers

"Maybe you will be a piano player like your Grandma,"

I whispered. Cradling her in my arms I stared and I stared, hoping one day she would know the intense love I had for her. "I want you to know how sorry I am for giving you away. You know it doesn't mean I don't love you." I swallowed hard as tears streamed down my face. "I love you more than my own life, and I know this couple will love you the way I do. They are expecting you, they deserve you."

I brought her close to my face, kissing her cheeks, soaking them with my tears. "Please believe I'm doing what is best for you. I am going to miss you so much." Whaling like a baby myself, I lay down, placing Mary Grace belly-side down on my chest, and cried myself back to sleep.

"Jane, wake up," Grace whispered, as she gently tapped my arm. I opened my burning eyes, and saw Grace standing over me with a desperately sad look on her face. "How are you doing, Jane? Are you okay?"

"No Grace, I'm not," I cried.

"I know, I know," Grace said as she wiped my eyes. "Here, let me take her." She scooped Mary Grace up off my chest and held her over her shoulder.

"I named her Mary Grace," I said. Grace smiled and instinctively began to rock back and forth as Mary Grace whimpered.

"That's a beautiful name." When I looked up at Grace's face I knew it was taking all she had not to break down herself. It was for my sake she was being so strong. "You're being discharged in a half hour, Jane. Maybe you ought to get dressed." I nodded in agreement.

Fully dressed, I lowered myself on the edge of the bed right next to where Grace was sitting. Mary Grace was cradled in the crook of her arm. My sister looked at me, tears pouring from her eyes "This is so hard" she cried, "I am so sorry you are going through this, Jane."

"I know," I said, leaning my head onto her shoulder. "We're both going through it." We both looked up at the door after hearing a knock. "Danny!" I exclaimed.. "What are you doing here?" My brother Dan was always there for me in my time of need, and even more than that. I had told Dan about my pregnancy shortly after I moved into Rachel Residence. I needed the support but kept who I told to a minimum.

"I came to be with you while Grace brings the baby down to the nursery." I immediately got up and went towards him, and he held his arms out and hugged me.

"You drove 600 miles for me?"

"Hey, what are brothers for?" he said as he rubbed my back.

I looked up at all six feet five inches of him. "Do you want to see her?"

Danny put his head down. It was almost as if he felt ashamed. "Please don't be hurt, but I can't. If I look at her I'll see her face for the rest of my life."

Grace stood up holding Mary Grace. "Jane, it's time." I looked at Grace, pleading with my eyes.

"Please don't let this be happening."

"I'll wait outside," Danny said, softly and sadly.

I began to feel my legs buckle. I quickly sat down on the bed. Grace handed Mary Grace back to me. My daughter gazed up at me blankly. As I looked down at her little face I could feel a burning ache in the core of my being. I didn't say anything. I just stared at her perfect face. I took my index finger and stroked her soft cheek. My teardrops began to fall onto her face. She blinked her little eyes with each drop that fell, and stared back at me as though she knew I was her mother.

"You need to say goodbye now, Jane," Grace said quietly. Still nothing, just tears. Grace leaned over to take Mary Grace from me. Crying herself, she placed her in the crib. She turned her head, so as to not look at me or Mary Grace, and began her journey down to the nursery.

I jumped up, yelling, "You will always be in my heart, Mary Grace. I love you!"

Hearing me weep uncontrollably, Danny quickly entered the room and held me until my last tear fell.

A nameless nurse wheeled me out of the maternity ward. Unlike the other mothers leaving the ward, I had no baby with me, my arms were empty. My heart felt vacated, I could not imagine feeling whole again.

Danny and Grace were waiting in Danny's car outside

the main lobby doors. As we approached the car, the nurse helped me into the back seat. "There you go honey, now put your seatbelt on, and good luck." Then she slammed the door. As we pulled away from the hospital, I looked back, knowing Mary Grace was still inside waiting to be picked up by Elizabeth. I wondered what her adoptive parents might be feeling; obviously excited, and hopefully grateful.

"You okay, Jane?" Grace asked as she turned around grabbing my hand. I could see Danny looking in his rearview mirror at me. They both felt my pain with me, without question.

"I'm taking it in the moment," I said with sadness. I remember dreaming of the day this would all be over, wanting so badly to have my life back, but at that moment, I'd wished I could go back and relive the last three days over and over again.

I was relieved to be going back to Rachel Residence, back to my friends and the sisters. I needed the little transition period before going back to my other life. Before we arrived there, Danny and Grace took me out to eat lunch. I have to say I played with my food rather than eating it. We finally approached Rachel Residence. My stomach was in knots because I knew I had to say goodbye to Grace and Danny. This was it—the final chapter of our journey.

"You will never know what you coming up here means to me, Danny."

"Sure Jane, it's where I wanted to be," he said as he embraced me.

"I'll see you next month," I said as I fought back the tears. "Thank Mary Beth for me, you know, for making it possible for you to come up here." Mary Beth is Danny's wife. She supported him supporting me through all my rough spots. She herself was another one I always was able to go to at any time, with any given problem. Love in abundance!

"We'll walk you into the house, Jane," Grace said.

"Honestly, this is where I need to break loose. Give me a hug right here."

"Okay, Jane, but here, this is for you. Read the note later." Grace handed me a small white envelope and a single pink rose. She leaned over and kissed me on the cheek. "I am so proud of you, Jane. I'll call you later." I could tell how upset she was. I watched both of them get into the car and stood there feeling empty and remorseful. I not only hurt myself, but I also hurt Grace, Danny, and all of the people that cared for me. Giving Mary Grace away was a loss for all of us. I knew at that moment that nothing would ever be the same again. I waved goodbye as they drove away, picked up my overnight bag, walked up the steps, and pushed the doorbell.

Sister Rita answered the door smiling. Standing there, I couldn't help but think of when I had stood there six months earlier, filled with anxiety and anticipation, and Sister Rita's smiling face staring back at me. It was the same scenario, same anxiety and anticipation, but of a different kind. As I stepped inside, Maria and Shannon were standing there to greet me. "

We're glad you're back," Maria said as she hugged me.

Shannon's hug followed Maria's. "It hasn't been the same without you here. Are you doing okay?" Shannon asked, trying to sound halfway cheerful.

"I am just about okay, and really tired. Please don't feel bad, but I think I'm going to lie down for a while."

Sister Rita chimed in, "I think that's a really good idea. Jane, you walk up those stairs slowly, and girls, you can help her with her bags."

"Sure," Maria said as she and Shannon followed me upstairs. The girls put my belongings in my room as I placed the rose and card Grace gave to me on my dresser.

"Thanks, guys, I'll find you when I'm done napping, maybe we can watch a movie or something later."

"That sounds good," they both said with sympathetic grins. They left and I shut the door behind them.

I began to weep and threw myself on my bed. "I want her back," I kept crying out, "I want her back."

The next thing I knew, I was opening my eyes. My room was dark. I must have slept for some time. Immediately my thoughts went to Mary Grace. Was it a dream? I thought as I sat up. Feeling the pain from the wounds, I realized it was no dream. I stood up to put the light on. As I did, a light from outside shined on my dresser. I glanced over at the rose Grace had given me earlier. After switching the light on I walked over to my dresser and picked up the envelope. I knew it would say something powerful, being that it was coming from Grace. I knew I should sit to read it. I lowered myself onto my bed and proceeded to open the envelope. The front of the card was covered with roses.

> Dear Jane,
> God's work manifests itself in so many ways. The rose in its simplicity symbolizes God's gifts of love, life, beauty and perfection as He sees them.
> You have given to Mary Grace the gifts of love, life, beauty and perfection, and she, in turn, has given you the gifts of love, life, beauty and perfection. Because of this mutual giving, that love can never be given or taken away. God said, "Give and you shall receive." I want to thank you and Mary Grace for showing me the true meaning of those words.
> Love, Grace

Naturally, I wept some more. I held the card and the rose for quite some time, knowing with so much longing for Mary Grace, along with my first feeling of peace since my journey began, that I would be okay, she would be okay, all would soon be well.....soon. In the days to come I was able to write a letter to my daughter. I decided it would only be fitting to share with her, the letter Grace wrote to me. Along with my letter and Grace's, I gave Mary Grace a silk rose.

Part Two

Surrender and Acceptance

Writing Part two was quite difficult to say the least. Many of my loved ones will be affected by this. The reader must try to keep in mind this is all of my loved ones' story but my perception and memory of it. It's raw, and it's real.

For my entire family
"All I ask of you is forever to remember me as loving you"

Chapter Ten

Seven years later

The basement apartment in Queens I shared with my husband Gene and son Paul was rather small. It had only one bedroom, which Gene and I thought Paul should have. Gene and I slept in the living room on a pull-out couch. The apartment had a spacious dining room whose floor was covered in gray indoor and outdoor carpeting. It was furnished with a three-legged table that leaned against the wall so it would stay standing, four chairs sat beneath it. That evening, Gene and Paul sat at the three-legged table, coloring, interacting beautifully, as always. I gazed at them thinking about what a good dad and husband Gene was. He was so young…younger than me, and so hard working. We may have had a tiny apartment and a broken table, but we were content; we were more than content, we were happy. Gene did his very best to provide for us, and I was grateful for that. Those feelings of happiness quickly turned to feelings of sickness. I found my way to the bathroom and proceeded to lose the dinner I had consumed the hour before. As I splashed cold water on my face I couldn't help but think of how nice pregnancy would be if I didn't spend half of it over a toilet. I brushed my teeth and went back to the couch to lie down.

"I'll put Paul to bed, hon," Gene said with a hint of sympathy.

"Come and give me a kiss goodnight, Paul." He ran to me and gave me a tight squeeze. "I love you, darlin'," I said.

"Night, mommy, bless you."

"Good night and God Bless you too, Pauly!"

I couldn't imagine loving anyone more than that little guy. About an hour passed before Gene came out of Paul's bedroom. Looking like he just woke up himself, he rubbed his eyes. "He finally fell asleep."

"And you finally woke up!" I said to him, giggling.

Gene plopped himself down next to me on the couch.

"What are you watching?"

"There isn't much on, so I'm watching "Towering Inferno," even though I'm watching it for the umpteenth time." I no sooner snuggled up next to Gene when the phone started to ring. "Can you answer it, pleeease?"

Gene picked up the receiver. "Oh, hey Kath, is everything all right?"

It was then I saw a look on Gene's face that I had never seen before. With his eyebrows scowling and his skin turning to a sheet white, he looked at me with fear. "Hold on one second Kath, Jane is right here." Gene placed the receiver in one of my hands and immediately took hold of the other.

"What's wrong, Kathy?" I asked with a shaky voice.

"It's Grace."

"What about Grace?"

"Mom just called." I could tell Kathy was crying.

"What about Grace!?" I yelled in a panic.

"She got sick yesterday with flu symptoms, no one thought too much of it. Mom went down to see if she needed anything from the store. Grace asked for ginger ale. By the time mom got back from the store and brought it to her, Grace couldn't speak. Mom called Tim at work. He came home, and she, Tim and dad took her to the hospital. She is in a semi-coma now, mom said she may die."

I sat there completely stunned, unable to say a word. I could feel the blood leaving my face, my heart pounding so fast it felt like it was going to explode. I sat there in silence for a long minute, but snapped back into reality at the sound of my sister's cries coming from the other end of the receiver. Immediately I felt the need to get some feeling of control in this. My way was to try and calm Kathy down.

"It's okay, Kathy," I said while Gene sat next to me rubbing my back. "I'm sure it's not that bad, maybe you heard mom wrong. In fact, I'm going to hang up with you and call mom and dad. Are you okay? Are you alone?"

"I didn't get it wrong, Jane, but you should call them any way. I'll be okay, John will be home in a bit, and the kids are here with me." John was Kathy's husband. He would undoubtedly be devastated to hear the news. He was so close to Grace. John and Kathy had four beautiful children; Johnny, 12; Kim, 10; Erin, 5; Kristi, 4.

"I'm going to call them now. Call me if you need me, otherwise I'll call you in the morning so we can make arrangements to fly up there."

"Yeah, okay," Kath whimpered, "talk to you in the morning."

I hung up the phone. My eyes met Gene's as I lifted my head. He was looking at me with such distress. "Why are you looking at me that way? She's going to be fine," I said with some anger and a lot of denial. I didn't know it was denial at the time, I thought it was the truth. I had to believe it was the truth. "Kathy and my mom have it wrong. Grace is not going to die. Do you hear me?"

"Okay, okay," Gene whispered as he continued to rub my back. "Just call your parents and see what they have to say."

I picked up the receiver. I stared at the numbers and couldn't for the life of me remember their phone number, a number I called nearly every day. My mind was blank—I was completely numb.

Gene saw the puzzled look on my face. He took the phone from me. "I'll dial for you." He dialed my parents and handed the receiver back to me.

"Hello, Mom? It's me, Jane. Please tell me Kathy made a mistake," I pleaded. There were a few seconds of silence.

"Oh, Jane, I was calling you next, honey," she said in a quiet trembling voice. "She's in grave condition, Jane. The flu went to her brain."

"Can she die, mom?"

"The doctors said there's still a chance she could survive."

"Oh, Mom!" I wailed out couple of deep sobs and then quickly snapped out of it. I couldn't stand the depth of my own cries. "Everything will be fine Mom, there is hope, let's hold onto it!"

"Yes honey, let's hold onto it, and pray, just keep praying."

"Of course we will pray, Mom. How are Dad and Tim and the children?

"Naturally, we're all completely beside ourselves. Dad's in bad shape. Tim's at the hospital with Grace, he wanted us to be with the children, which I think is best, too. He'll call us during the night if anything changes for the worse. Dad and I'll be going back up there first thing in the morning."

"Okay. Please hug them all for me. Try to get some rest, Mom, I'm worried about you. I'll call you in the morning. I'm sure we'll be flying up there tomorrow. Love you, Mom."

"You too, honey, God bless you."

"God bless you too, Mom."

As I hung up the phone I couldn't help but think about how composed my mother was. It wasn't because her heart wasn't being torn out, but she worried about everyone else. She chose to be strong for us, always had, it was amazing. At that moment I pictured my parents sitting in their home at the kitchen table, maybe praying, or just sitting there in excruciating pain, never in a million years guessing anything like this would happen while they were alive. After all, they moved up to Tim and Grace's thinking they might need assistance in their older age. It's the very reason Grace wanted them to move in with her on her property.

Poor Mom, Dad, Tim, and the kids. This just could not be happening, not to our family, not to my sister. For a quick moment I actually thought of there being no Grace, of her dying. Quickly, I turned that nightmare off in my head. Coming back to the moment, I noticed Gene staring at me again as he continued rubbing my back.

"Go on now, Jane. Go get ready for bed; I'll set up the couch for us."

"Yeah, okay," I whispered, then in a rather robot manner I worked my way to the bathroom to wash and change. When I came out of the bathroom, I saw that the bed was ready for me. Our pillows were fluffed up, the blanket turned down. There was even a box of tissues on the end table next to my pillow. That was Gene, always trying to make everything right.

Gene came out of the kitchen. "Go lay down, hon, I'll be right there. Can I get you anything, maybe a cup of tea or something?"

"No, I'm good." I climbed into bed, pulled the blanket up to my chin, and turned on to my side. I could hear Gene walk up the stairs, undoubtedly to make sure the door was locked, then back downstairs and into Paul's room to check on him. A few moments later I felt him get into bed. He snuggled up next to me and began to rub my shoulders; in turn, I began to cry, and I cried for a very long time.

I woke up to the familiar soft breath of Paul on my face. I opened my eyes and saw his dark chocolate eyes looking back into mine.

"Morning mommy," he said with a smile.

"Hey honey, come on in, under the covers." He scooted his little body in next to mine like he did every morning. My stomach felt especially sick that morning. As I stroked Paul's head, the reality of what had happened the night before hit me, which made my stomach even sicker. Was it a nightmare? Please let it have been a nightmare, I thought. That's when I spotted the crumpled up tissues all over the end table from the night before. It was real. The panic hit me once again. My heart began to race, and the pit I felt in my stomach felt like it was going to devour me from the inside out. I wanted it to; anything but face what might be awaiting me and my entire family.

I rolled over and began to shake Gene. "Gene, Gene, wake up." He grunted, not an unusual sound coming from him — he did it every time I tried waking him from a sound sleep.

"We have to talk. Wake up Gene. I have to start planning to leave."

"What?" He sounded annoyed.

"Gene, wake up. Remember last night? Grace?"

He sat right up, rubbing his eyes, "Oh, I'm so sorry."

"No, it's okay. I actually thought it was a bad dream when I woke up."

Gene pulled me to him, hugged me and kissed my forehead, then leaned over me to kiss Paul's. Proceeded to get out of bed, he said, "I'll make you some toast. Hey buddy, how 'bout some Cheerios? C'mon, give me a hand."

Paul rolled out of bed and followed Gene into the kitchen. He was like his little shadow. I propped myself up in the bed, reliving all that had transpired the night before, weakening more with each thought. Before I knew it Gene was standing before me with a plate of toast. I forced some of it down. I ate it only because I knew I needed to. I sat there not knowing what I was feeling, basically numb, until the phone rang.

"I'll get it," I said, leaning toward the phone, filled with both eagerness and fear.

"Hello, Jane, it's me, Kath."

"Any news?" I asked hesitantly.

"I just spoke to Dan, who spoke to Dad. She's worse, Jane, her kidneys are failing," she cried. "We need to fly up there today." I sat there rocking back and forth feeling like my heart was being ripped out of my chest. "Dan is going to make the flight arrangements. I'll call you when I know more," she said in a monotone voice.

"Okay," I murmured, barely even able to get that word out.

Gene looked at me apprehensively. I stood up to walk towards him, and then felt my legs go out from underneath me. I wound up on my knees and once again began to rock back and forth, shaking uncontrollably. I couldn't stop. Gene came towards me and began to help me up. I resisted his help and began to push him away, as if he represented my pain. I had to push this evil nightmare away. He grabbed hold of me. The more I resisted, the harder he held onto me, until I finally gave in and yelled out a cry that I never cried before.

"Gene, I can't lose her, I can't live without my sister." My sobs got deeper and louder until I couldn't stand the sound anymore, and I abruptly stopped. Gene helped me to my feet. "Okay. I'm okay, and Grace will be too," I said aloud, trying to convince myself and Gene. I could tell by Gene's face that he wasn't convinced. I then looked over at Paul, forgetting that the poor baby was witnessing all of this. With his eyes speaking volumes of compassion, he looked at me, ignoring Sesame Street, which was now blaring in the background.

"It's okay honey, Mommy is okay."

"You're sad, Mom."

I walked over to him, knelt in front of him and grabbed hold of his little hands. "You're right Paul, I am sad. Aunt Grace isn't feeling well and I am worried about her. I'm going to go away for a few days and see her, maybe that will make her feel better."

"All right," he said, then gave me a hug and gave his attention back to Bert doing "the pigeon."

I looked back over at Gene. "Do you think your mom can watch Paul while you're at work?"

"Don't even think about all of that, I'll take care of it. Just do what you have to do to get ready to go. Leave everything else up to me." Then he hugged me.

Chapter Eleven

The evening came quickly considering how awful and tortuous the day was. There were phone calls back and forth; hopeful news, bad news, hopeful news, then bad news again. There was a knock on our door; my signal that it was time to go.

"Jane, Kathy and Danny are here."

"I'll be right there, Gene!" I shouted as I shoved the rest of my belongings into my suitcase. As I put my coat on, I had to remind myself of where I was going, as it still was not real to me. I stepped out of the living room to find Danny and Kathy standing at the bottom of the stairs. Seeing the despair on their faces was too much to bear.

"Oh, Danny." I walked towards him and fell into his arms.

"It's okay Jane, it's okay," he said, rubbing my back. Kathy stood by whimpering. I broke away from Danny's embrace to hug Kathy. Beautiful Kathy, with her angel face and long dark hair, she even looked pretty when she cried. I wrapped my arms around her and pulled away quickly. As I looked at her she reached her hand up to my face and gently wiped away my tears.

"Ooh, your hands are cold." I sniffled. We both smiled softly.

"Let's get going you guys, you can't miss that plane," Gene said loudly with a crack in his voice. That was Gene, always trying to break the mood when it was somber or held any hint of anger. The three of them went up the stairs and out the door. Following them, and about to shut the door behind me, I realized I had forgotten something. I ran back downstairs and took the rose Grace had given me several years before out of its vase, wrapped it in a paper towel, and placed it in my bag. When I got outside, Gene was standing outside the car, waiting to help me in. As I slid into the car, silence filled it. Fear was radiating through all of them, and I couldn't help but feel their fear as well as mine. As we pulled away, I looked back at the house we lived in, knowing regardless of how things turned out, nothing would be the same when I returned.

"I spoke to Chris about an hour ago." Kathy's voice startled us after a long stretch of silence. "She spoke to Mom. She said Grace's hands were getting warm, it could be a good sign."

"That's great!" I shrieked loudly, with hopeful enthusiasm. "Why didn't you tell me when you came into the apartment? That means there's still hope." Danny and Kathy both stayed silent, I guess in order not to encourage me, or discourage me either. Except for some necessary exchanges, we were quiet for the rest of the trip to the airport and the entire flight. We were all speechless.

Exiting the plane, I could once again feel that burning pit in the center of my stomach. I purposely walked in between my siblings just in case I felt the urge to collapse, which I feared wasn't far from happening.

"There's Robert," Kathy said as she pointed. Robert was a close friend of Grace and Tim's, whom I knew quite well.

"I guess he's here for us," Dan said. It was obvious to all of us in looking at Robert that it wasn't good. His normally rugged complexion was now pale white, with sadness written all over it. He began to briskly walk towards us.

"Hurry, we have to get to the hospital quickly, things are getting worse by the minute." Nothing else was said, we were all in our own zone. It was awful. We followed him with bags in hand to his car, got in and drove with him on that dark rainy night to the place of dread.

Pulling into the hospital parking lot I gazed up at this tall, now scary building, the building Grace had worked at for years as an assistant head nurse in the adolescent unit. I looked up at the windows, most of them lit, knowing in each room lay a patient with their own story. I was sick with the thought of Grace laying in one of those rooms fighting for her life. I could barely stand up as I got out of the car. I was literally shaking like a leaf. One foot in front of the other. Looking down at the puddles on the concrete, I took one step at a time; each leg feeling like it weighed 100 pounds. I just didn't want to face what I had to face.

I managed the journey into the hospital and it felt like the longest, hardest walk of my life. We entered the elevator.

Robert pushed the button, "#7 I.C.U." As the elevator doors opened, all I saw were people, familiar people, filling the corridor. As we walked past them, I could feel their eyes staring at us. I even heard some soft whispers. It wasn't until much later that I realized they were all there for Grace. Some of them were longtime friends, some were co-workers of her and Tim. We were quickly directed by one of the nurses to go to the family room. "Two more doors down on the right," she said sympathetically.

As we entered the room, I saw Tim sitting there alone. His eyes were swollen shut, his handsome face covered in dark blotches. His man-tailored shirt's collar was unbuttoned, and was wrinkled down to the tails that hung out of his pants. I could see he hadn't slept. He gazed at us with such longing, a longing for us to take his pain away. Danny walked over and put his hand on Tim's shoulder. As he did I could see his shoulder begin to go up and down. He began to sob, almost violently; it was the most grief-stricken I had ever seen anyone, something I never wanted to witness again. We all took turns hugging Tim. He just sat there crying, shaking his head in disbelief.

"It's just incomprehensible, how am I ever going to go on without her?"

"Where are the children?" asked Kathy.

"They're home with your parents. They insisted on staying, but I convinced them to go home for a few hours to get some sleep."

"I want to see her. Can I see her? " Danny asked with urgency.

"Of course you can, Dan. She's in room 724." Dan headed towards the door.

"Danny, she doesn't look like herself." Dan continued out the door. Kathy and I took a place on the couch on either side of Tim. I took one of his hands in mine. He looked up at me.

Taking turns looking at each of us, he said, "You are good sisters, good sisters." We all sat there quietly for a minute, when Kathy broke the silence. "I think I'm ready to see her now."

"I'll go with you," Tim insisted as they both stood up. "Are you coming, Jane?"

"Not yet, in a little bit." I just sat there alone, frightened like a little girl. I eventually felt strong enough to get up. I walked out of the room and looked down the hallway, where I saw Danny leaning against the wall with his face in his hands. I knew he was crying. I began to follow the signs to get to room 724; it seemed like another endless journey. Trembling with anguish, I kept hearing Tim's words "it doesn't look like her."

The sign for room 724 hung on the wall to the left of a large window. The window was covered with blinds, probably to block the view of passersby to the patients. As I entered the room I saw Kathy next to the bed and Tim beside Kathy. I stood there staring in utter disbelief. My beautiful sister was lying there hooked up to every machine imaginable. I slowly walked over to Grace's bedside and took hold of her cold, lifeless hand. Mustering up strength, I raised my eyes to look at her face.

Her eyes were open, not because she was conscious, but because the swelling of her brain forced them open. Tubes were in her nose, and a ventilator was taped to her mouth. The feeling was beyond surreal, and yet I was able to take notice of my senses. The sounds of those machines, the deep sobs of my sister Kathy, and the sight of my precious sister's still and lifeless body looking nothing like the angel we all knew. It was all too much to bear.

"This can't be Grace," I said, then began to feel my legs give out on me. A nurse standing by me caught me before I hit the floor.

"Come on, honey, let me get you to a chair." I could barely put one foot in front of the other as the nurse, Tim, and Kathy escorted me out of the room into the hallway.

"She's pregnant," whispered Kathy to the nurse.

"Here, sit down now," the nurse said. "I'll get you some water." Out of the corner of my eye I could see Tim walking back into the room. He was so zoned out, he looked like a robot. I'm sure we all did. Kathy stayed with me, rubbing my back and crying at the same time.

As the nurse returned with some water, Kathy asked, "Will you be all right here?"

"Yes, Kath. Go ahead back in, I'll be right there."

"You probably should go home and get some rest," the nurse said with concern.

"I'll go soon. I want to be with my sister for a while".

"I am so sorry for you and your family. I don't know Grace, but a good part of the staff here does. I heard she is an amazing person and an outstanding nurse. I have heard nothing but wonderful things about her. Everyone here cries with you."

I stared back at her in a daze, dropped my face into my hands, and sobbed. "Oh, sweetie, it's okay. Can I get you something else?" the nurse asked as she stroked my head.

"No, it's okay. I'm okay." I took a deep breath and reached my hand into my pocket for a tissue. "I could use a tissue."

She reached into her own pocket and handed me one of hers "It's clean. And I'm Sara. Please, if you need anything, I'll be here all night."

"Thanks, Sara, I'm Jane, and I'll let you know."

"Please, call on me for anything. I'm guessing that was your sister that told me you were pregnant. When is your baby due?"

"In October," I said, sniffling. "Three days ago I couldn't think of anyone else but this baby, now I feel nothing."

"You're in a state of shock. Best thing for you right now is rest. Your baby needs you to rest."

"I know, soon."

I would go in to see Grace every few minutes over the next two hours, but could only stay in the room maybe two minutes at a time. I couldn't stand it. I know I did the best I could. Reluctantly, I took a ride home with Grace and Tim's friend John. Danny and Kathy insisted that I go. I agreed it was the right thing to do, and I did want to be with my parents. As we pulled into the driveway, I could see that the lights were still on. I was sure dad was sitting up waiting for me.

"Thanks so much for the ride, John."

"It was no problem, Jane. Do you want me to walk you to the door?"

"Oh no, I'm fine. Looks like my parents are up waiting for me. I guess I'll see you in the morning?"

"I'll be up at the hospital first thing. Please give your folks my best, and let them know I'm available if they need me for anything."

"Thanks, John," I said as I shut the car door and waved goodbye.

When I walked up the steps to their door, I could see through the glass, Mom standing in her bathrobe, and Dad still fully dressed, but wearing slippers instead of shoes. The door opened to both of them standing there. "Hi Jane," Dad said softly, barely able to look up at me. I knew he was afraid he would break down.

"Oh Dad," I cried and then fell into his arms.

"Okay, okay." He patted my back. "It's okay."

"I'm sorry, Dad." I pulled myself from him. I looked over at my Mom. She looked back at me with pursed lips, shrugging her shoulders and fighting back the tears. I knew her so well. The warmest, softest women I ever knew, but always the strongest when it came to being a rock for her children. We hugged for a moment.

Glancing over my mother's shoulder, I saw Grace's children, all in sleeping bags lined up on the floor.. Looking at them lying there, I couldn't help but feel guilt. I was so wrapped up in the thoughts of what the loss of Grace would do to me, I wasn't thinking of them or my parents as much as I should have. There I was, standing in my parents' home, and they were losing their baby. I couldn't fathom anything happening to my Paul.

Then there were Grace's children. I was blessed enough to have my parents' support through this nightmare. These babies were losing their mother. Oh my gosh. How could I be so self-absorbed? "You need to get some rest, Jane. Why don't you get yourself ready for bed?" my mom whispered.

"Yeah, okay, I know. You need your rest, too. Have you even slept?"

Dad stood there with his head down. Mom answered, "Very little, but trying, just trying."

"Well, all right, I guess I'll go lay down. Please wake me if the hospital calls."

"Sure, Honey," Dad said. I watched him walk toward the

door to lock it. My dad always looked years younger than his age. He was a tall man, physically fit, and had silver hair and the complexion of a man in his fifties. What is this going to do to him? The thought of it sent shivers down my spine. I got ready for bed with great effort, knelt down, said my prayers, and climbed into the sofa bed my parents had ready for me. I lay there wide awake with memories of Grace flooding my head and heart. What really got to me was the thought of there only being memories of Grace left. Once again, I began to cry. Moments later my mother walked into the room, she must have heard me crying. She sat herself down onto the edge of the bed. I looked up at her. "Mom, there is still some hope, isn't there? We need to pray for her to live."

She looked back at me despairingly. "Of course. We can all pray for her to live, but more importantly, we need to pray to be able to accept what God's will is for Grace."

There was silence. I turned on my side, and my mother then began to rub my forehead in a circular motion with her thumb, like she did when I was little. Then I fell asleep.

Chapter Twelve

I woke up to the sounds of the telephone ringing and my mother's voice.

"Hello? Oh, hello, Dan. Yes, ohhh, okay then, we'll be there shortly. Thank you, honey," she said softly, her voice trembling. I jumped out of bed—not a smart move. I had to sit right back down, I was so lightheaded. I sat there for a moment, and then stood up slowly. I went and turned the light on; it was still dark. I looked at the alarm clock that was on the night table. It was 5:15. I heard my mother from where I was standing.

"Danny said they took another brain scan. There's no longer any brain activity. We have to meet up at the hospital to decide as a family what to do."

I looked out the door into the kitchen to see her holding herself up with one of the kitchen chairs. My father sat in his usual seat. With tears already streaming down his cheeks, he began to sob. That was only the second time I had ever seen my father cry. The first was when his mother died. My mother walked her way around her chair, and pretty much fell into it. Oh, please, God, this can't be happening. I looked over at the living room where the children had been sleeping. All four of them stood there with sleep still in their eyes, just staring in disbelief; not a word was spoken from them.

৵৹৻

When we reached the seventh floor the elevator doors opened to the corridor filled with many of the same faces, only they looked even more disheveled. Wearing the same clothes and looking exhausted, I could tell many of them never even left. As we walked into the family room, we found Kathy curled up on the couch covered with a hospital blanket. Her sweater was bunched up beneath her head, and she was sound asleep. In a chair next to her sat Danny, looking extremely uncomfortable. He was snoring with his head back and to the side. Looking at them, I was glad I went home for a couple of hours sleep, and I was glad my parents did, too. I worried so much about my mom, having survived two heart attacks and bypass surgery. I was frightened of what that might do to a woman of 65. Dad was strong and healthy, but being over 70, who was to say what losing Grace would do to his health?

"Should we wake them?" whispered my mother.

. "I think they'd want us to."

Kathy started to stir at the sound of my father's voice. "I'll be back in a bit. I'm going to see Grace," I said. With my head down, completely zoned out, I walked down the hall to Grace's room. When I entered her room I found Tim draped over Grace's body, crying hysterically.

"Rabs, you can't leave, please don't leave," he cried. Rabs was Tim's nickname for Grace. I didn't know where or how he came up with that name for her. I always found it endearing, but not that day. That day it sounded pathetically heart-wrenching. There was another person, the love of her life that had to be without her. He turned around and saw me at the corner of his eye, then pushed himself up off of Grace. He started to walk towards the door.

"No, Tim, please don't leave," I pleaded.

"No, I'm all right. You spend some time with your sister," he said as he walked out of the room.

I reached into my purse that hung over my shoulder and walked toward Grace. I pulled my hand out of my bag, and in it lay the rose, half wrapped in a paper towel. I took the rose, lifted Grace's swollen hand off of her stomach, and placed the rose underneath it.

"Love, life, beauty, and perfection as he sees them. If you only knew just how much I appreciate all you have done for me, and how much I love you. I can't imagine life without you Grace," I cried, "please watch over my girl, our girl. I'm going to miss you so much." My sobs got deeper and deeper. I couldn't take anymore, and ran out of the room. I saw my parents, Danny, Kathy, and Tim walking toward me to go to Grace's room. I turned and ran the other way. I wanted to be by myself. They called out for me but I didn't answer. They left me alone; they knew it was what I needed.

I slowed my run down to a walk and found my way to an

empty waiting room. I went in, shut the door, and took a seat on one of the two brown leather couches that were in there. I remember sitting and staring at the carpet on the floor. It had a pattern like a maze, beige and brown, and it made me dizzy. I saw myself walking through that maze as if it signified my life. I followed one of the lines with my eyes until it came to a dead end, which snapped me back into the moment. I felt as if I was coming to that dead end, as if I was dying. I almost wanted to, the pain was so bad. I truly didn't think I would survive Grace's passing. I began to think about my other siblings, wondering when the rest of them would arrive. Surely Billy, Tommy and Dave would be arriving soon. I assumed they would arrive together, as they all lived in close vicinity to each other, and about 200 miles south of Grace's. My concern was for my other sisters, Tess and Chrissie. Both of them married West Point graduates, and they were stationed far away.

Tess and her husband Bob were stationed in Germany, and Chrissie and her husband Billy were stationed in Hawaii. I couldn't stand the thought of them not making it in time to say goodbye to Grace. My heart ached for them, but I held on to the hope of them arriving in time. I had to. I continued to sit there for some time, appreciating the silence and being alone with my thoughts. I finally decided it was time to get up and call Gene.

As I walked back toward the family room, where I knew there was a payphone. I spotted my three brothers coming out of the elevator. Looking back, it surprises me that I was able to see them in the midst of the crowd that was there, and they were all there for Grace. Tommy and I had exchanged eye contact, and I could see from a distance that he was saying "There's Jane" to my brothers as he pointed to me. We began to walk towards each other, all of my brothers wearing solemn faces, and immediately I began to cry. Again.

"She's not gone, is she, Jane?" Tommy asked fearfully as Billy and David stood by waiting for the answer.

"No, she's not. I don't know what you heard last, but as of a few hours ago, they talked about turning the machines off. It's really bad guys," I said while shaking almost uncontrollably. It was hard enough to think of it, but to say it was so much worse.

"Oh, God." David began to weep. At that point, no one knew who should console who, we all just took turns hugging.

"Where are Mom and Dad?" Billy asked eagerly, "and the children?"

"Mom, Dad, Kathy and Danny are with Tim in Grace's room. The kids will be here soon, they're with friends."

"Where is Grace's room?" Billy asked.

"Just go to the end of this hall," I said as I pointed, "and make a right. She's in room 724. Guys, I'm warning you now, you will hardly recognize her. She looks awful, nothing like herself," I said while I continued to shake. "I'll be there in a few minutes, I have to call Gene."

"Sure. Will you be okay by yourself?" Tommy asked.

"Yeah, I'm good," I lied. I wished someone would carry me to the pay phone. It took such great exertion to stand up, never mind walk. I'm sure seeing my brothers and their pain made it even more real. The pain got worse with every family member I saw, which I didn't think was possible. I watched my brothers walk down the hall, none of them speaking. Bill and Tommy's arms were on Dave, who was walking in the middle of them, whimpering. I made my way to the family room and began to dig in my purse for change. After gathering only 50 cents, I decided to call collect. I dialed 0, then my home phone number.

"Hello, operator. How may I direct your call?"

"Yes, I'd like to make a collect call from Jane."

"One moment, please."

The phone rang and rang. "Please pick up, Gene. Please pick up." I pleaded to no one. I looked at the clock on the wall, it was only 9:00 a.m. Gene had left for work. I'll have to try him at lunchtime, surely he'll be at his mother's to check in and see Paul. Oh, how I needed to hear their voices.

"I'm sorry, no answer. Maybe try again later," the operator said.

"Okay, thanks," I responded before I hung up the phone feeling defeated. I knew it was about time I went back to see Grace. I dreaded it, because as much as I wanted to be with her, it was so overwhelming to see her the way she was laying in that bed. As I left the family room, I saw Michael and Barbara, and approached them.

"Hey kids," I said as I hugged them. Little Barbara, just nine years old, hugged me back. Michael tried to, but couldn't. His 18-year old body had no strength. Those poor children; Barbara was still a baby, and Michael, he was so close to Grace, she was his confidant. They would sit alone in the morning and have coffee together before he left for high school and she left for work. I really believe that Grace was not only their mother but was also a true friend to all of her children. That was Grace—so approachable, and always filled with words of wisdom.

"Where are Bethany and Marie?" I asked with concern.

Michael answered, "Bethany went down to Mom's room, and Marie was afraid to come, she's with her friend Erin's family."

"Do you want me to walk with you to see your mom?"

"Not just yet, Aunt Jane," Michael said.

Barbara nodded. "I can't right now, maybe in a little while."

It's amazing how differently all of us are handling this agonizing situation, I thought. All of us feeling this heart-wrenching pain, and all walking through it however we could. I thought of Marie, 12 years young, afraid to come, poor sweetheart. I totally understood. I was 26, and I could barely stand up. Then there was Bethany, approaching 15 and already in the room with Grace. Michael and Barbara were trying to gain the strength to go in to see her. We were all just barely walking the walk, all of us in our own way, surviving.

"Do you want to sit down kids? How about some water? Did you eat?" I asked, trying to distract them (as if I could).

"We're good, Aunt Jane. You go ahead and see Mom. I'll take Barbara into that room you were just in. We'll sit for a while."

"Sure, honey, I'll be back in a bit," I said. I started to walk toward her room. All I could hear was chatter around me from the tons of people lining the hallway. I felt so guilty not speaking to any of them. I knew several of them, just couldn't carry on any conversation. As I approached Grace's room, I spotted my Dad, Tim, my brothers, and Kathy outside her door.

"What's going on, why are you out here?"

Dad said, "Bethany is in there. She's reading a letter to Grace, Mom is in there with her. We all figured we would give them that time together." We just stood there with our heads down. There were no words, only feelings of complete torture. We waited there a while, and then went back in the room. Once again the sounds in her room went right through me. The beeping of the machines, the noise of the ventilator, which at that point was my sister's lifeline. The chilling sound of my family's debilitating cries.

Seconds after we gathered around Grace's bed, an unfamiliar nurse came into the room. "The doctor would like to speak with the family. Considering the size of your family, his suggestion was that you all go into one of the meeting rooms. It isn't as intimate as the family room, but at least you'll all be able to have a seat when the doctor speaks to you. If you follow me, I'll show you the way."

Feeling overcome with despair, I followed her and the rest of my family out of the room. We dropped Bethany off to be with Michael and Barbara. Thankfully we found Grace's friends hovering over them, making sure they were taken care of, a huge help to us in those horrible hours. We arrived at the meeting room, which was small, but big enough to fit a large buffet length table in it. One by one we took a seat at it. As the doctor started to speak, all of us looked up at him; some with fear, some with sadness.

"I am really sorry about what has happened to Grace. I want you to know that the entire staff here is deeply saddened by what has happened to her. I've known Grace for years. She was an outstanding nurse, an incredible person. She was admired by all who knew her here. I don't know if all of you know the seriousness of Grace's condition. It appears she had the flu. So, 99 percent of people that are stricken with the flu get influenza A. One percent gets influenza B, one tenth of one percent die from it. Grace has influenza B, and she falls under that one tenth of one percent. She has no brain activity at all. You can keep her hooked up to the machines, where she will always remain in a vegetative state, or you can slowly turn off the machines and let God take over."

You could hear a pin drop, until Tim broke the silence. "Well, I think we all feel the same way, don't we? We all know Grace would never want to stay in this state."

I couldn't believe those words were coming out of his mouth, but I knew he was right. We all did. I looked over at my parents. My dad was sitting in his typical position, arms folded and head down. My mom just sat there with tears pouring out of her eyes.

The doctor cleared his throat. "Well, alright then, I'll give you folks a few minutes together. Tim, I'll have the nurses get the paperwork in order. I'll be with you in a bit. Again, I am truly sorry for all of you." He walked out of the room.

What could be said in those moments? I only remember Billy suggesting that we pray the "Our Father." We all held hands, some of us prayed the words, while some wept them. After praying, a few of my siblings departed from the room. I recall a few words of exchange between who was left there, though I don't remember what they were. I remember sitting there in such complete shock... and yet it was real to me because the agony accompanied the shock. It was the strangest feeling, if you can call it a feeling.

My thoughts eventually went to Gene and Paul. I looked at the clock and saw it was 1:20. "He has to be at his Moms, I thought as I excused myself from the table and left the room. After finding my way to the pay phone, I decided I wouldn't bother searching for change again, and would call collect. I finally reached him. "Gene?" I leaned up against the wall. I remember wishing his arms were there to collapse in, because I felt like I was going to.

"Hey babe, how is everything? I've been waiting for you to call."

"Oh Gene, she's going to die, she's going to die today." I fought back the sobs with all of my might so that he could understand me.

"Oh no, I'm so sorry." I could tell he was starting to cry.

"They're unplugging the machines today. She has no brain activity at all. Oh, Gene, please get here, I need you to be here," I cried.

"I'll get on the phone with the airlines now. I'll call you back. How is everybody, your parents, Tim, the children?"

"We're all barely standing, it's horrible, Gene. How is Paul?"

"He's okay, he's happy being with my mom."

"Can I speak to him?"

"My mom left a note for me saying she was taking him to the toy store and then to Burger King, they haven't come home yet."

"Are you bringing him with you?"

"It's up to you. Aunt Mary said she would watch him if I needed to go up to be with you. I think it's best that he stay back, he's so little to be involved in all that. I think it would be better for you and for him if he stayed with my mom or Aunt Mary. He's so content with both of them."

I pictured him with both of them. Gene's mother, fixing him blueberries and waffles and singing to him, Aunt Mary getting right down on the floor at eye level, playing anything his little heart desired. He loved being with both of them, and I felt such comfort in that.

"I agree, but please explain to him that I'll be home soon, and please hug him and kiss him for me."

"Of course I will. I'll call you when I have the arrangements made. I love you and miss you. I'll be there soon, just hang in there, hon, and give my love to everybody."

"Okay. Bye, Gene." I hung up the phone and found a seat. Again, I just sat.

❧❦

About one hour later

The scene in Grace's room was surreal to say the least. Standing at the head of the bed was my dear mother looking down at her baby, stroking her forehead like she did to mine the night before. "It's okay Grace, you can let go now. God is waiting for you."

At the other side was my brother Billy, praying the "Our Father." My dad sat in a chair in the corner, unable to move or say a word. David stood facing one of the corners of the room. The sound of his cries will never escape me.

Danny stood at her feet, rubbing her leg and saying, "You are going to get to meet God first." Kathy and Tommy were standing at her bedside crying. I felt like I wasn't there, like I was a separate entity, it was so bizarre.

At that moment, Tim collapsed, draping himself over Grace's body. Then he passed out. The nurse who was adjusting the machines reached ever so calmly into her pocket and pulled out smelling salt and placed it under his nose. She helped him up. It was so pathetic.

"This is happening now, Tim. Do you want to be in here?" the nurse asked quietly.

"Yes, I'm okay, yes," he said, completely out of it. We all stood by and watched as the nurse slowed the last machine down. We watched as the ventilator machine went up, then down, then up, then down, then up, then down. Then it stopped. That was it. It was over. Our Grace was gone. Nine days later, so was the baby I was carrying.

Part Three

Angels Unforeseen

Hopefully we are all aware of the angels in our life.
Sometimes it isn't until we are going through a difficult time,
are we aware of their presence. In my heart, I hope all of those
that have surrounded me know who they are and what they
mean to me, even those I have never met. Thank you!

For Tommy and Conner, and Billy
"The will of God will never take you where the Grace of God
will not protect you."

Chapter Thirteen

Twelve Years Later

There I stood in the same salmon-colored bathroom, only it wasn't as repulsive to me yet. I stood over the sink with my heart pounding, waiting anxiously for a plus or minus sign. I stared down at the thermometer-looking gadget and watched as the blue horizontal line was crossed with a vertical line.

"It's a plus, we're pregnant. We're really pregnant!" I leaped into Gene's arms. He giggled and swung me around. I freed myself from his embrace and looked into his eyes, touched by the water pooled up in them.

"When should we tell the kids? Oh my goodness, I am so excited!" I exclaimed as I jumped up and down like a little girl. Gene stared back at me; he didn't need to express his feelings with words. I could see the joy in his eyes and smile.

"I don't know. When do you want to?"

"Oh gosh, I don't know, but I want to tell them in a special way. Let's videotape it!"

"Yeah?"

"Yes, I know they'll be thrilled." I was referring to our two children, Paul who was now 14, and Gracie who was nine.

Paul grew up to be a handsome young man, quite tall for 14, with dark hair, dark semi-slanted eyes, and a contagious smile. He loved his instruments; drums being his first instrument, the bass guitar his second. He excelled at both. He was also great at most sports. His studies took fourth place over those things. His social life naturally took first, as it would with any typical 14-year-old. Gracie was our little girl, and what a sweetheart, named after my precious sister. With her golden curly locks reaching the middle of her back and her huge sparkling blue eyes, she brought so much life into every room she entered. She was an exceptional dancer, as good as Gene, (did I mention Gene was a great dancer?), and I would watch her with such pride as she consistently did her dance moves throughout our house. Gracie was wonderful with babies and desperately wanted us to give her a brother or sister.

Well, it was really happening, and immediately my wheels started spinning on just how we would share our wonderful news with our children. Gene and I stood alone in our kitchen, which Gene had just completely renovated. He did major structural work, including putting a steel beam in to replace a supporting wall he knocked down. I think it took about 25 men to bring it in the house. I don't know how they did it. Anyway, our living room and kitchen were now one big room. Gene did such a beautiful job. Tin covered the ceiling, while hard wood covered the floors. Raised, white panel framed the sage walls. A black marble-covered island separated the sitting area from the main kitchen, which had cherry wood cabinets and stainless steel appliances. It even had a silent dishwasher. We had come a long way from our three-legged table and pull-out couch for a bed.

I looked over at Gene, "Are you ready?"

"Yup, ready," he answered.

"Paul, Gracie, we need to speak to you," I shouted up the stairs where they were both hopefully doing their homework. It seemed like an eternity before they both finally came downstairs and plopped themselves on our rose-print settee.

"What, ma? Can we make this quick? I'm in the middle of something," Paul said, rather impatiently.

"Well, it can't be as important as this," I answered.

"It can't be as what important as what? What's the camera for?" Grace asked as she looked into its lens and made funny faces into it.

"Well, dad and I have a question for the two of you. We need your opinion. Out of the two vacant rooms we have upstairs, which one of them should we make the nursery?"

They both looked at us, puzzled for a moment, and then I saw the look on Paul's face. He got it.

"What?" he giggled, "You're having a baby?"

Gracie shrieked with excitement, "Oh my gosh!" Her eyes pooled up with water just like Gene's did when he found out. She began to jump up and down on the couch. I didn't stop her. I was overwhelmed but not surprised by her enthusiasm.

Paul smiled from ear to ear, hugged all of us, and said, "That's great, guys," and proceeded to walk up the stairs, still wearing his infectious smile, a smile that was worn with complete sincerity. Life at that moment was beautiful. As soon as we shared the wonderful news with our children, we immediately began making phone calls to our families. I was always good at keeping secrets or surprises from people when I was supposed to, but this was neither, it was just fabulous information that I wanted to shout out to the world.

I called my parents first.

"Hello, Mom, it's me, Jane. Guess what?"

"Oh. Hi, dear. Is everything okay?"

"Yeah, everything is great. Gene and I are having another baby."

"Oh, Jane, that's wonderful," she said in her sweet, soft voice. "Paul and Gracie must be delighted."

"Grace is flipping out. You know Paul, he doesn't say much, but by the look on his face when he found out, I could tell he was happy."

"Wait until I tell Dad. How are you feeling, and when are you due, honey?"

"I'm feeling fine so far, but it's early yet. The way I calculated it I'm due on July 17th."

"Oh, you are really early."

"Mom, it isn't like it used to be, you can take a test the day after you miss your period. I only missed mine about five days ago. I could barely wait the five days. You know how patient I am."

My Mom giggled. "I'm pleased so for you, Jane. Wow, another little cherub to add to our family, I can't wait." Her voice went up in pitch, which it often did when she was really happy. I knew she would be. You would think that my parents having 28 grandchildren already would lessen the excitement of a new arrival. Not with my parents, they embraced each grandchild as if it was the first one born.

"When will you be going to the doctor? You know you need those vitamins," She commented with a non-authoritative tone. My mom was never one to push her opinion on any one, or be at all controlling. She gave her

opinion only when it was asked for, that's the truth. I wish
I had the same attributes. I talk way too much. Sometimes I
have to literally put my hand over my mouth in order to not
voice my opinion on a certain subject. I take after my dear
old dad that way. I loved him dearly, but he was definitely
opinionated, and he'd be the first one to admit it. I knew in
my heart what Dad's opinion and feelings would be regarding
mine and Gene's pregnancy, and that he would be genuinely
elated.

"Don't worry, Mom, I'll be calling the doctor to make an
appointment this week. I'd love to speak to Dad, is he there?"

"No, honey, he's at the senior center playing pool." The
senior center was a lovely place for the local patriarchs to go.
Many senior citizens would gather there for several different
activities, or even just to sit and talk. The center also had its
own band, which my mother played piano for, sharing her gift
of music as she always did. My parents never ceased to amaze
me. They were 80 and 87 and still extremely active, sharing
themselves and their talents. I believe that's why they stayed
so youthful. "Do you want me to have him call you so you can
tell him?"

"No, that's okay, Mom, you can tell him." She would
never say it, but I knew she wanted to tell him. She was like
me in that regard, or should I say, I was like her. We loved to
share good news, especially with my dad. At that point Gene
was standing over me. I could tell he was eager for me to hang
up so that he could tell his own mother.

"All right then, mom, I'm going to go now. Gene is
anxious to call his mom."

"No wonder! Please congratulate Gene and the children
for us. I'm so happy, and I know Dad will be. Please let me
know when your doctor appointment will be."

"Sure thing, Mom. Give Dad a hug for me. Love you."

"Love you too, honey. Bye."

I hung up the phone feeling very content. Gene sat down
next to me on the couch. "Okay. I'm putting the speaker phone
on," Gene said. He knew me so well. God forbid I didn't hear
my mother in-law's reaction.

"Hello?"

"Hey ma, it's me."

"Hey baby, what's up?"

"Did you say just say baby? That's what's up, Jane and I are gonna have a baby."

"What?" She shrieked.

"We're havin' a baby," Gene said with a huge grin on his face.

"Oh my God, we are happy about this, right?" she asked with a nervous laugh behind it. Gene and I both knew she didn't mean that in a negative way. No feelings were hurt, she happened to be a very practical person, so it didn't surprise us that she that she asked that question. She was just making sure before she showed us any type of emotion either way.

"Of course we are," Gene and I responded simultaneously.

"Oh, thank goodness," she said with relief. "I'm so happy for ya, kids. I bet my Paul and my Grace are excited."

Grace leapt into the room when she heard her grandmother's voice. "I'm ridiculously excited."

"I bet you are, baby" she chuckled. "You'll be a terrific big sister. This child will be lucky to have you, but remember baby, you will always be my special." That was something she said to both of our children, and she meant it with each one. In her eyes they were both special to her in their own unique way.

"I know, grandma," Grace said, beaming. She was bouncing up and down. I could tell it was hard for her to contain herself.

"Jane is making an appointment with the doctor this week. We'll let you know when it is."

"Okay kids, I'll let Kenny know. Can I tell Mary?"

Kenny was her soon-to-be husband, a great guy and a wonderful grandfather to our children. Mary was Gene's younger sister. Being five-foot ten, blonde, blue eyed and, gorgeous, she turned heads everywhere she went. Having the vivacious personality that she did added to the attraction. She was newly married to Frank, a hard-working, friendly guy. He was crazy in love with my sister in-law, and Mary's feelings were mutual. I knew Gene wanted to tell Mary, but he didn't want to take that away from his mother. He was so much better than me when it came to things like that.

"Sure, ma, you tell her."

"I'll do that right now, she'll be so happy." There was a pause. "Okay kids, love ya's."

"You too", we all chimed in, grinning from ear to ear.

We spent the next hour or so making phone calls to let everyone know. Of course, my brothers and sisters were the next to be informed. I had to call all but one, because they all lived far away. Naturally they were all pleasantly surprised and very excited. My sister Kathy was someone I wanted to tell face to face. She moved into an apartment adjacent to our house after a sad divorce. Unfortunately, Kathy worked late that night so I would have to wait until the morning to tell her. I did refrain from telling three of my dearest friends as well. They lived close by and I wanted to tell them in person. I decided I would pay them a visit sometime the next day.

After completing all of our phone calls, it was time to prepare dinner. I decided to fix something light and quick, as Gene had planned to attend a meeting at our local fire department. He joined the fire department as a volunteer nine years before. Gene always wanted to be a fireman, and although it took him away from the family more often than I approved of, it was important to him, and it was definitely one of the many things he was called to do in his lifetime.

He didn't just go on fire calls. He also went on ambulance calls along with the E.M.T.s. I remember one particular call he went on that I was witness to, which happened to be in the apartment complex we lived in four years prior. It wasn't an unusual call — an elderly woman with chest pain. I watched from a distance as they wheeled our poor neighbor out on a stretcher. With her frail body covered in a white sheet, her tiny head was all you could see. She was grey haired and had an oxygen mask over her face. I watched Gene as he walked bent over alongside the stretcher, wheeling her to the ambulance. Although I couldn't hear what he was saying, I could see he was talking to her. I saw the true compassion in his eyes as he stroked her head. It was a scene that would be forever embedded in my heart and mind. I still get crazy sometimes when he runs out the door during a meal or if we had prior plans, but more often than not, I flash back to that call, and it centers me.

We all sat over a dinner of rice and beans and very pleasant conversation. We were all so happy. "What are we going to name the baby?" Grace asked, still beaming.

I looked on smiling as Gene commented, "Oh Gracie, we have plenty of time for that, but that's not to say we can't pick up a book of baby names and start looking."

I chimed in, "I think that's a great idea. I'll go to the book store tomorrow and buy one." Gracie continued eating, appearing to be quite satisfied about the idea of a name book and her plate of rice and beans. Paul did as well, but more so with his rice and beans.

We finished our meal. Everyone helped clean up, even Paul, who typically tried to escape from doing the dishes. It had to be all of the positive energy in the room that made all of us so ambitious. My ambition didn't last too much longer, however. I could feel the fatigue start to hit me. I don't know if it was all of the excitement that transpired that day, or if it was because the sure signs of pregnancy were already making themselves known.

Gene left for his fire department meeting when I decided to get ready for bed, but not without saying goodnight to the kids, who were both upstairs in their rooms. I climbed the flight of stairs with great effort; I was so wiped out. I went in to Paul's room first. We fixed his room just the way he wanted it. Gene built him a bed that you step up onto. The step was wide enough to be a seat and surrounded the bed, which was a platform. It was covered in grey Berber carpet. The walls were a slightly dull cobalt blue with two broad grey diagonal stripes going down each wall. He had a framed Beatles poster hanging on one of them. I believe the one from "Let It Be." An acoustic bass guitar dangled from one of the walls as well. Paul also owned an off-white electric Fender jazz bass, and a light aqua electric guitar, both sitting in stands under the two windows on the far wall.

Paul was lying on his bed reading one of the books from the Harry Potter series. "Good night, babe. I'm going to bed," I said as I tapped on his opened door.

Paul instinctively got up and kissed me goodnight. "Good

night, ma," he smiled, "I'm really happy about the baby."

"Thanks Paul. I still can't believe it. Don't stay up too late. God bless you, Paul."

"God bless you too, Ma." He threw himself back on his bed and continued to read.

I went to Grace's room, the room I dreamed of as a child. Grace and I came up with the color scheme, and she gave me a few ideas of what she wanted. Gene and I surprised her with her room being completely redone after returning from a two-week visit she had with my sister Chrissie, brother-in-law Billy, and nieces Jamie and Shannon down in Alabama. She flipped when she saw it, and it was no wonder, it looked like a life size dollhouse.

Her bedroom was almost too big for such a little girl to have, but I was happy she had it. Peach and off-white striped wall paper went two thirds of the way up the wall, which ended at a two-inch cream colored chair rail. Above that was a delicate floral print wall paper, which complimented the stunning light blue and cream-colored dental crown molding. Gene actually painted each tiny little square in the crown molding.

There were two large windows in her room, and lace curtains cascaded from each one. In between the windows was a mock fireplace, beautifully hand crafted by Gene. Two framed photos rested on its mantel. One was of her, taken at one of those glamour studios. I had actually worked there doing makeup a few years before. Her hair was up in a twist, and she had a feather boa wrapped around her. She looked too mature for my taste, but it was taken all in fun. The other photo was of her and my nieces, Cassy, Kathleen, Shannon, and Janey. It was taken outside of our swimming pool. They all were wearing swimsuits. With wet hair, and their arms around each other, they smiled back at the camera. I loved that photo. You could see how happy they were to be together. Standing at her doorway, I found Gracie writing in her journal, undoubtedly expressing her joy about her new brother or sister. She was lying on her light shag carpet belly down, propping herself up with her elbows.

"Hey Gracie, what are you doing on the floor?" I asked

with curiosity. Gracie looked up at me, appearing a bit startled.

"Oh, Mom, I didn't hear you coming. You scared me."

"Oh, I'm sorry. You looked pretty involved with your writing there."

"Yeah, I'm almost done. I had to write about what happened today. It was a big day."

"It sure was, and one day you'll look back at what you wrote and remember the happiness this day brought you. I think it's wonderful that you're writing about it."

I looked at Grace in amazement; she was so mature in so many ways. There she was all of nine years old, and she was journaling. I was so pleased that she appreciated the many benefits of writing, as I did.

"Well, Gracie, I'm going to bed now. I told Paul he needed to go to bed soon, and I'm trusting that you'll do the same. It's 8:30 now; I'd like you to be in bed by 9:00. Now, come on, and give me a hug."

"Love you, Mom," she said as she hugged me. Then she put her thumb on my belly and did the sign of the cross "God bless you baby, in the name of the Father, the Son, and the Holy Spirit. Amen." I was shocked, but then again, I wasn't. She learned it from my sister Tess, who would bless her own children every time they left the house. I started to bless mine as well, but must confess I wasn't as consistent with it. Gracie, however, was very consistent. She blessed our baby every night from then on.

"Thanks, Gracie. You are amazing! Good night now," I said as I rubbed her back. She found her way back to her floor and continued to write.

I walked to the other end of the short hallway, to the other two bedrooms that were upstairs. They were directly across from each other, just as Paul's and Grace's rooms were; only there was a bathroom on the far wall in between them. I glanced into the smallest of the bedrooms, which had just about room enough for a crib, a dresser, and maybe a rocking chair. I imagined myself in that rocking chair, holding an infant swaddled in a blanket. I didn't imagine what gender the baby was, it didn't matter. All I knew was that the image thrilled me beyond belief, and somehow made me feel complete. I did an about face and walked over to the other bedroom, which was about three steps away, and switched the light on. It was an empty room that happened to be Paul's before we redid his new room. I never thought of moving our bedroom upstairs, but now it would be time to. I looked at the slightly marked-up grey walls and weathered carpet, knowing the renovation of that room would be mine and Gene's next project. It was exactly what Gene would want to do—rip another room apart. I mean that with all sincerity; he always needed a "project" to work on. Now, he would have the nursery, our new bedroom, and our soon-to-be former bedroom to renovate. Nothing would make him happier. Boy, did we have a lot to do in the next eight months.

I went downstairs, locked the doors, and got myself ready for bed. I knelt as I always did to say my prayers, thanking God for the many blessings of the day, and most especially for our pregnancy. I climbed into bed, feeling particularly grateful for the comfort of it, being as tired as I was that evening. I laid there with an exuberant amount of joy and pure excitement, which you would think would have kept me awake; on the contrary, it knocked me right out. I never heard Gene come into our bed. He actually had to wake me up the next morning. It was usually the other way around.

Chapter Fourteen

After a breakfast of French toast with syrup, Gene left for work, and the children were off to school. Of course, Grace practically ran out the door. She couldn't wait to get there to tell her friends and her teacher about the baby! Shortly after everyone left for the day, Kathy made her usual morning visit. She tapped lightly on the door, and came in. She was dressed in her purple scrubs. Every day it was a different color, depending on what the day of the week it was. It was not by choice, but her job's dress code. She worked in an orthodontic office, and a very busy one at that. Her commute was lengthy and her hours were long. I felt like she was never around.

"Hey Jane" she said, looking pretty happy, perhaps because it was Friday and the next day was the one Saturday she had off a month.

"Hey Kath, how was work yesterday?"

"Long, but okay. I don't think my head hit the pillow before I fell asleep last night. What are your plans today?" she asked, as she sat down on one of the stools at the island.

"Same old stuff. Cleaning the house, then I may hit Borders. I also have to call the doctor."

"What's wrong? Do you feel okay?"

"I feel fine, and nothing is wrong, actually everything is right."

She looked at me puzzled. "What do you mean?"

"I'm pregnant!"

Kathy leaped up off the stool and came toward me, hugging me tight. "Oh my gosh, that's so great. Oh my gosh, I'm so excited. Gene and the kids must be flipping." I stood there giggling at her excitement. I was so happy that she was so happy.

"They are thrilled, Kath."

"Who knows so far?"

"Pretty much everyone knows but our friends. I didn't call you last night because I wanted to tell you in person. I hope you aren't upset."

"Are you kidding? Why would I be upset? Did you call my girls?"

"No, I would never let them know before I let you know. I actually left it up to everyone to let their kids know. Otherwise I'd still be on the phone. I figured you would want to tell them anyway."

At this point her children were a lot older, John was 28, Kim, my Goddaughter was 25, Erin, 19, and Kristi, 18. They were sure to be pleased by the news, as we all were with any new addition to our family.

"Oh good, I think I'll go back to my apartment now and call them. You don't mind, do you?"

"Of course not, I've got to get moving anyway. Tell them all I said hello."

Kathy couldn't get out the door fast enough, but not without turning to me before she walked out. "Oh my goodness, I didn't even ask you how you were feeling, and when are you due?"

I smiled at her "I'm fine Kath, a little tired, but I think it's all the excitement. As far as my due date goes, I calculated mid July — July17th to be exact."

"Wow, your wedding anniversary."

"Yup!" I said, pleased that she remembered our anniversary.

"Well, feel good, and take it easy today. Have a great day."

"You too, Kath. Have fun telling the kids." She walked out the door very happy. I was glad I had something to do with it!

I cleaned up the breakfast dishes, made the beds, showered, and then called my friend Patty to ask her if I could stop by to talk to her for a few minutes. Patty and Kevin were two of our dearest friends. Gene and I met them shortly after Gene joined the Fire Department. I actually met Patty before I met Kevin. She was in the Ladies Auxiliary with me. I had joined one year after Gene joined the department to support him, and also to meet his fellow fire fighters' wives. Anyway, back to Patty. I instantly took a liking to her. She was so friendly, but in a subtle way, not overpowering. Her sincere warmth was overpowering, in a good way. It radiated around her. Patty and I felt an instant connection to each other. We immediately began to share our feelings on many things, finding that our shared faith was our common bond.

Patty and Kevin had known each other since elementary school, and started dating in high school. Patty being a cheerleader, and Kevin a star basketball player, they made the perfect high school couple. They both continued on to college, and eventually married. Patty later became a special education teacher. Unfortunately, the day before her twentieth birthday, years before I met her, Patty was diagnosed with an illness called Scleroderma. Most people diagnosed with this dreadful illness are in their late thirties and forties. I can't imagine the fear and pain that Patty, her parents, Kevin, and entire family must have gone through with the news of her disease, especially at her young age. The prognosis was not good, as this illness can be potentially fatal. Scleroderma is a group of rare progressive diseases that causes the hardening and tightening of the skin and connective tissues. Some of the symptoms that go along with this illness and that Patty herself experiences are the drying up of tears in her eyes, disfigurement, chronic pain, loss of fingertips, lung disease, mental strain, and others. The amazing thing about Patty is that you would never know there is a thing wrong with her. She is a beautiful woman (though she always argues that) who truly never complains about her daily physical pain, which can be extremely severe, and frequent. She is the type of person who is always there for those who are in need, not just those who are dear to her, but strangers as well. Of course, she is heavily involved in the Scleroderma Foundation, and is a Scleroderma Tri-State Board member.

When Patty was diagnosed with this illness, she was told she shouldn't have children, as giving birth could be detrimental to her health, and in all probability make her illness progress quicker. She and Kevin then made the decision to adopt a baby. After much research into the adoption process, they decided to try to adopt a child from Romania. Patty and Kevin were blessed enough to have been able to adopt quickly. Six months after beginning the process, Michaela was brought home to America. What a gift, a beautiful baby girl! I believe Michaela was around three years old when I met Patty. What a doll, she had a flawless olive complexion, big dark eyes, and dark hair. Well, shortly after

I met Patty, she and Kevin gave Michaela a little brother. Yes, Patty became pregnant and gave birth to little Kevin who was born six weeks early. Two beautiful children, when she never thought she would have any. Thank God her health remained basically the same; not great, but not worse.

Now it was time for me to share my wonderful news with her. I drove over to her house, which was only a three-minute ride. Patty and Kevin owned a beautiful home; it reminded me of a castle. It was all grey slate. The front door was red and had a round arch at the top. It sat in on about an acre and a half of property, which was impeccably manicured by Kevin. The property in the back of the home was three tiered, and had a stream running through it at the very bottom; it was truly breathtaking. There were two doors you could enter in the front of the house. I always went to the one that led into the sunroom. I knocked, and heard Patty shout, "Come on in, Jane."

I opened the door to her two Scottie dogs barking at my feet. Although I don't dislike animals, I am not one to fall all over them. I pet them quickly, looked up, and saw Patty standing in her kitchen on a stepladder.

"What are you doing? Can I help you with something? I asked with concern. She turned around to me laughing her contagious laugh.

"I was organizing my cabinets; you know me, I have to have everything in its place, and I need this stool because I don't have your long legs!" She laughed again.

"You want to come over and organize mine?" I said as I laughed. I'm going to have to be doing a lot of organizing with the baby coming and everything." I waited for her reaction; it took a second.

"WHAAAAT?" she screamed as she always did when she was excited. "You're pregnant?" She immediately stepped off the stool and came over to give me a hug. "Oh, I can't believe it, a baby, I'm so excited. What did Paul and Gracie do when you told them? How's Gene? I bet he is elated."

I looked back at her, satisfied by her enthusiasm. As I said before, Patty was a very attractive girl; she had thick, dark, medium-length hair, cut to frame her face. She was tiny

in stature, had dark brown eyes, high cheekbones, and a tiny
nose, which I envied (Not really). Looking at her I could feel
her excitement for me, and I could see it in her pretty brown
eyes.

"We are all delighted beyond words."

She grabbed my hand. "Sit. Let me make you a cup of
coffee. Will you have some coffee? It's decaf. Have something
to eat. How about a nice roll with butter?" That was Patty,
"Miss Hospitable" to everyone who walked through her door.
You had to feel at home when you were there.

"Oh no Patty, I just ate breakfast. I can't stay for long. I
just had to tell you in person."

"Oh please stay for a bit, have a cup of coffee. Colette is
coming over. She would love to see you."

Colette was Patty's sister, she looked so much like Patty,
although her hair was a bit lighter, and her eyes were green.
She had three beautiful children, and was a cancer nurse at a
well-known hospital, not too far from our town.

"I'd love to see Colette. Okay. One cup of coffee, decaf,
as long as it's no trouble. Where is your mom, is she coming,
too?"

Patty was named after her mom. Pat was an extremely
faith-filled woman with a dynamic and funny personality. Her
daughters took after her in stature and in the ability to bring
so much positive energy into a room. While I'm on the subject
of her family, I have to mention her father Mike, and brother
Michael. Mike was a gentle, loving man, and very handsome.
I told Patty he looked like an older version of Ben Affleck.
Michael was also like his mom and sisters; full of personality,
and good looks. He was married to a lovely girl named Dana
and had two beautiful children.

"She isn't coming today. She and my dad are going over
to my Aunt Sharon's house for lunch."

"Oh, you'll have to tell her about the baby for me," I said
while helping Patty by placing flowered coffee mugs and milk
and sugar on the kitchen table. Colette arrived shortly after
the coffee was done brewing. Naturally, she was excited to
hear about our pregnancy. We had had about 30 minutes of
pleasant conversation over our decaf and rolls, when I decided

it was time to go. I said my goodbyes and went on my merry way.

I stopped at the bookstore to buy the name book I promised Gracie, and then at the supermarket to pick up some ground beef to make American Chop Suey for dinner. That was a dish my mother used to make when we were kids. It went a long way and was a favorite of ours. When I returned home, I completed my household chores, and then rested a while before Paul and Gracie returned home from school. They were both always hungry when they came home, so I often prepared a special snack for them. Paul's started turning into more of a meal. Most of the time he requested two garlic grilled cheeses. Gracie preferred something lighter, like a toasted English muffin with cinnamon. I felt blessed to be home for them. In that day and age, not many couples could afford to have one parent home. That isn't to say I didn't work outside of the house, because I did. I worked for my Godmother Jane, as one of her assistants. She was a well-known food stylist. I would only assist her on large commercial jobs, mostly for a famous pizza chain. I worked approximately six to eight times a year. The days were long, and the jobs lengthy, so I would stay with Jane, and her husband Mitch, for the duration of the jobs. They were always extremely hospitable to me. I was grateful for these jobs because the pay was incredible, and comparable to what I would bring home if I had a part-time job all year round. I was also very grateful to Jane and Mitch for always opening their home to me.

Needless to say, Gracie was thrilled with the book, and started thumbing through it immediately. She began to shout out names as she sat at the island while I prepared dinner. "How do you like the name Isabella for a girl? Or Hannah?" Gracie asked.

"Those are both cute names. We'll have to go through the book together. Do you see any boys' names you like?" I asked with my eyes filled with tears, only because of the onion I was chopping.

"What do you think of Aiden?" She asked, almost sounding puzzled.

"Um, I'm not so sure I like that; it's a nice name, but I like more of the old fashioned names. We'll keep looking through it, we have plenty of time, sweetie. I'm sure we can come up with a name we all like. In the meantime, do you mind setting the table for dinner?"

"Do I have to?" she whined, while she slid herself off the stool.

"It would be helpful, Grace. You can look at the book again when you are done. I want to eat early tonight. I'm leaving you with Paul while dad and I run over to Kelly and Larry's quick. I want to tell them in person that I'm pregnant."

"Ohhhh, that's so good, Aunt Kelly is going to be so happy."

"Aunt Kelly" was another close friend of ours. Gracie referred to both Kelly and Patty as aunts, because she felt close enough to them to do that, and they felt like family to all of us. I agreed with Gracie that Kelly would be so happy, not just for us but for her and her husband Larry too. Kelly was also expecting, so as fate would have it, we would go through this journey of pregnancy together. We ate dinner shortly after Gene arrived home from work. We chatted about the day's happenings while we finished up our meal and cleaned the kitchen. I rushed through it, because I was anxious to get over to Kelly and Larry's to tell them the good news.

"Be good to Gracie while we are gone, Paul. No teasing, and Gracie, no instigating."

As good as the kids could be, leaving them alone sometimes meant trouble. Typical sibling rivalry would occur. "We'll be fine, Mom," Paul said as he as he gave Gracie a smirk. I think he did it on purpose. He knew how to tune me. Gene and I left, and I departed with some reluctance and also with a bit of hope that peace would reign over our home until we returned, which would probably only be about an hour.

We pulled up to Kelly and Larry's home. Their house sat one third of the way back on their acre of property. They owned a cape; it was very pretty, with doghouses that expanded from the second floor windows. Beautiful flowers lined the driveway and the walkway, while a floral wreath hung from their door. It was so welcoming, but not even close

to as welcoming as it was when you entered their home. Gene
and I knocked on the door, waiting patiently, knowing they
weren't expecting guests at that hour on a weekday. Andrew
answered the door. Andrew was their 11-year old son, a
delightful boy, and as warmhearted as his mother.

"Oh hey, come on in."

"Hi Andrew," we both said. "Are your mom and dad
here?"

"Yeah, Pop is upstairs and mom is getting laundry from
downstairs. She should be right up. I'll run up and tell Pop
you're here. I don't know what he's doing up there."

"Okay," Gene said, "tell him not to rush." Andrew ran
up the stairs two to three steps at a time. Gene and I stood
waiting for both of them. Kelly came around the corner with
a basket of laundry in hand. She wore her long blonde hair
in a ponytail on top of her head, and she had a t-shirt and
sweat pants on. In the six or so years I had known her, I had
never seen her dressed like that. Kelly was always impeccably
dressed from head to toe. It was actually refreshing to see her
dressed down; she still looked great!

"Hey guys, what are you doing here? Oh my gosh, you'll
have to excuse my appearance, and the house. I just got home
from work a little while ago. I got right into my sweats. My
clothes are getting a little tight on me, looks like it's finally
time to hit the maternity store," Kelly said, giggling. Gene
immediately went over to her and took the laundry basket out
of her hand.

"Let me get that for you. Where do you want it?"

"Oh thanks, Geno. You can put it right on the coffee table
there."

We could hear Larry running down the stairs, and he
jumped into the room, all six feet of him. He was wearing his
fire department t-shirt and jeans. Larry was pretty well built,
with short dark hair and a mustache. I recalled his mustache
looking crooked once, and I mentioned it to him. It became
a standard joke between the two of us from then on. "Geno,
Janeth, (Silly nicknames of ours). What's up?" Larry asked as
he came over and gave me a kiss on the cheek. Kelly followed
suit.

"We're so sorry to be popping by like this, unexpectedly. We know you're probably tired, Kel."

"Don't be silly, is everything okay though?"

"Well, yeah. It looks like we could go maternity clothes shopping together," I said while Gene and I stood smiling waiting for a reaction. Kelly's face lit up immediately, while Larry still looked puzzled. Kelly then began to jump up and down.

"Oh, I can't believe it. This is so great; we're pregnant together."

Larry finally got it, and gave us a smirk. They both came over and embraced us.

"Guys, come in the kitchen. Let's make a toast to celebrate our babies. You girls can toast to juice, Gene and I will have a beer. You'll have a beer with me, right, Geno?" We followed them into the kitchen.

"Sure, I'll have a quick beer, but we can't stay long, we have to get back to the kids," Gene said as he gladly took a bottle of beer from Larry's hand.

"What will you have, Jane?" Kelly asked, as she stood by the refrigerator.

"Just a glass of water is fine. Thanks, Kel." We sat down at their kitchen table. It was a butcher-block top with white legs. There were navy blue placemats on it, and a pretty blue, yellow, and white bowl sat in the centre of it, filled with fruit. The bowl matched the wallpaper on the walls perfectly. White cabinets hung on the walls, and there were many of them. Each had silver, round knobs. It was such a bright and charming-looking kitchen. Kelly really had quite a knack for decorating. One room was prettier and more inviting than the next.

"How do you feel, Jane?" Kelly asked, with sincere concern.

"Wait, wait" Larry interrupted. "Let's make a toast." Kelly and I smiled and raised our glasses of water, while Gene and Larry raised their beer bottles.

"Here is to our beautiful wives, Kelly and Jane, and to our babies. Let the journey together begin!" Kelly and I looked at each other; I'm sure both of us thinking the same thing. It was a little corny, but a sweet sentiment just the same.

"Awwww. How nice Larry, good way to score brownie points," Gene commented while laughing.

"So, how are you feeling, and when are you due?" Kelly asked me with curiosity.

"Believe it or not, on our wedding anniversary, July 17th, at least that's what I calculated."

"Okay. So it's not too far from my due date, maybe four months?" Kelly was due the end of March.

"Well, we can muddle through a few months together anyway. Either way, they will be close in age. How awesome is that?"

"Oh my gosh, I can't tell you how thrilled I am," Kelly said with sincerity.

At that point, the guys had tuned us out and were in their own conversation, undoubtedly something about the firehouse. "Have you told Terri and Frank?" Kelly asked.

"No, I haven't yet. I drove by their house today. Terri wasn't there. I'll probably wind up calling her when I get home. I feel bad, but I don't think we'll have time to stop on the way home; the kids are alone, you know?"

"Yeah, of course, Terri will understand."

Terri and Frank were another couple we often spent time with. Again, Frank being in the firehouse is what connected us. They were a lovely pair. Terri was a sweetheart, and we really felt blessed to have each other as friends. As couples, we all got along famously, which made for a rich and pleasant social life. With all of us having fairly young children, we would often gather at each other's homes and socialize while the children played. Occasionally, we would go out dancing together, which was always a blast.

"So when are we going maternity clothes shopping?" Kelly continued.

"Whenever you're available, just let me know. I'm hoping it will be a while before I'm wearing them, but I'd love to take a look, then we can grab some lunch or something."

"It sounds good to me. We'll hit the mall. There are a few good maternity stores there. How does this Saturday sound?"

I looked over at Gene. "Excuse me, Gene. Kel and I are going to go shopping Saturday, is that okay with you? Do you have any plans?"

"That's fine," he said "I don't have anything going on."

"Great, then Saturday it is."

We finished up our beverages, and our pleasant visit, and were on our way back home. When we arrived there, we saw that all had remained well while we were gone, thank goodness. Paul was in his room playing guitar, while Gracie sat in the den watching television. I spoke to both of them for a bit, then made my phone call to Terri and Frank. Naturally, they were happy to hear of our news. At that point I was pretty tired. I said my goodnights to everyone, leaving them all awake, and retired to my bed.

Chapter Fifteen

One week passed before I called my obstetrician's office to make an appointment.

"O.B.G.Y.N., can I help you?" a woman asked.

"Oh, yes. Well, I'm pregnant, and I would like to make an appointment to see my doctor," I said nervously. I don't know why I let people on the other end of the phone, who I didn't know, intimidate me. How silly.

"Okay. Who's your doctor, honey?" she asked sweetly. With relief for her kindness, I responded

"Oh, it was Doctor Martino. I don't know if he's still there." Doctor Martino was a small, odd-looking man, with a high-pitched voice, and no bedside manner whatsoever. I had no choice in which doctor I had. I had to accept whoever they gave me, in the clinic we belonged to. We had an H.M.O., and unless we went outside the clinic for all of our medical care, including Pediatrician, and our G.P., I had to accept whatever O.B. they gave me. The truth was that I was quite satisfied with the other doctors, so I decided to suck it up and stick with whoever they chose for me.

"Oh yes, he's still here. Will you hold on one moment, please?" she asked.

"Sure, no problem. Thank you," I responded.

As I waited for the receptionist to get back on the phone, I stood in the corner of my kitchen, leaning against the wall, feeling tired and very sick to my stomach. I leaned over to one of the stools that sat at the island, the cord on the phone barely reached, but I managed to drag it toward me. I pulled myself up onto the stool and breathed a sigh of relief; I actually felt faint. I leaned forward, placing my head on my forearm that rested on my legs, while holding the phone's receiver with the other hand. I could feel the sweat beading on my forehead.

"Hello, hello?" I heard in the distance. "Hello, are you there?"

"Oh yes, I'm here" I said with effort. "I'm sorry. I'm feeling a little woozy."

"Are you okay?"

"Yes, I'll be okay, I'm sitting now. I feel a little better. This isn't unusual for me," I said softly. "Do you think you need to come in to see the doctor today? Otherwise the soonest we can see you is three weeks from today; we are pretty booked up."

"No, three weeks will be fine."

"Are you sure, honey? You don't sound very good."

"Honestly, I'm okay. I just need to eat something. As I said, this isn't unusual for me, but thank you for your concern."

"Okay then, November 30th, at 4 p.m., does that work for you?" She asked.

"That will be great."

"What's your name, honey?"

"Jane Spiotta."

"Okay then, Jane, you're all set. We'll see you on the 30th. I hope you feel better."

"Thanks so much for your kindness. Have a nice day."

"Uh-huh, you too. Bye now"

I waited a few more moments before I stood to hang up the phone. After a little snack of toast and juice, I started to feel much better. That was just the beginning of a long nine months of fatigue and nausea, but it was well worth it!

It seemed like an eternity for the three weeks to pass, not only because of the excitement of going to the doctor for my first prenatal visit, but also because I had spent most of the three weeks on the couch, with the exception of the necessary chores I had to do to keep the house at least a little presentable. Gene and the children helped me out a lot. I was really sick. The only things I could keep down were grapefruit juice and melted American cheese on toast. The moment finally came for us to leave. I made arrangements for Grace to stay with Patty while we went to the doctor. Paul opted to stay home by himself. As we drove to the Center, I began to flash back to all of my other pregnancies. My first child, Mary Grace, then to Paul and Grace, and of course, to the baby we lost. All the pregnancies held such mixed feelings; all had hope for a good outcome, even through some of the hardship.

We made our way into the office, and got called in two seconds after we sat down. One of the nurses held the door open for us and walked us to another office. She told us to take a seat and that the doctor would be with us shortly. "I wonder why they didn't bring me to an examining room," I said as I looked over at Gene.

"That is strange, right?" Gene said as he looked back at me with a puzzled look.

"Maybe they're just gonna take a urine test and talk to us." I hated the idea of an internal, but was anxious to know that everything was alright. Just then there was a knock at the door, and the doctor entered the room.

He held out his hand. "So you think you're pregnant?"

"Well, I know I am," I replied. "Either that or I have had a really bad stomach flu for the last few weeks, besides, the home pregnancy test I took came out positive," I responded, laughing. Gene joined me in laughter. The doctor didn't.

"Mmhmm, well, you'll have to take another urine test while you're here."

"No exam today?" I asked.

"No, next visit," he said as he plopped himself down behind his desk. "When was your last normal period?"

"It was on October 11th." I couldn't believe his lack of personality, and even more so his lack of interest. He barely even looked at us.

Gene just sat there not saying a word; he too was overwhelmed by the doctor's obvious emotional detachment from us. Neither one of us expected him to be falling all over us, but a little eye contact would have sufficed. He sat playing with a little cardboard wheel, trying to figure out my due date.

"July 17th," I blurted out.

He looked over at me, annoyed. Gene glanced over at me as well, with a disapproving look. I guess I was being rude by blurting that out, but I couldn't help it. The way this doctor was treating us was unacceptable in my eyes. I showed a little of the vindictive side of me that afternoon. Oh well.

"How old are you?" he asked. He glared at me.

"I'm 39," I said proudly

He cleared his throat. "Well, you know you need an amniocentesis."

"I am not having one," I snapped back at him. Poor Gene,

he was the innocent bystander. He knew where I stood with this doctor, and where I stood on the idea of having an amnio. Gene wouldn't put his two cents in at this point. Although he was one to always stand up for what he believed in, he knew I had this situation under control. He needn't have said a word.

"You're at high risk for having a baby with Down syndrome."

"Well, I'm not having an amnio. I know having one is a risk to our baby. Besides, if I found out there was something wrong, I wouldn't do anything anyway."

He cleared his throat again, which was now becoming annoying. "First of all, the risks are beyond minimal. And I think you should start thinking from your neck up, rather than your neck down. You don't know what these kids with Down syndrome are like. I have a cousin with Downs. When my wife and I got pregnant we decided if we were having a baby with Down syndrome we would have nothing to do with it. They are the type of kids who hide behind their mother and they will never go to college. If the child was on the fifth floor and the radio was too loud, they would jump out the window rather than turn the radio down. They are just retarded enough to know they are stupid."

With our mouths dropped open, Gene and I stared back at him in complete disbelief. We were speechless. The silence lingered for a moment before I finally broke it.

"I have no response to that spiel, except to tell you once again that even if there was something wrong, we wouldn't terminate the pregnancy, anyway."

He looked at us with disgust and said nothing. This time Gene broke the silence. "Jane is right, we wouldn't do anything anyway, but if there were something wrong it would be good to be prepared. Is it possible to see on a sonogram, if there's a problem?"

"Not always," he said with a hint of hostility while writing out a script.

"Here's a prescription for your vitamins, and also a script for the lab to have your urine test. You can make another appointment with the receptionist." He handed Gene the little slips of paper and we left. He clearly couldn't wait for us to leave, and the feelings were mutual. Gene and I walked past the reception desk with a noticeable amount of agitation.

"Aren't you making another appointment?" Gene asked.

"Not now," I said, "I'll call from home to make one. I have to get out of here."

"What about the urine test?"

"Okay, okay, I'll go for the urine test, but we already know I'm pregnant." I wasn't being very pleasant. Gene didn't deserve the nasty tone I had in my voice. "I'm sorry, Gene, he just really ticked me off."

Gene didn't look at me or acknowledge me; he was deep in thought the entire walk to the lab. I stayed silent. At least I did until we were finished in the lab and made our way to the car. Once I shut the car door, I'd had enough, and I broke my silence.

"How could he say things like that? He helps bring life into this world," I said loudly. "Ughhh, he makes me furious. How do we know we aren't having a baby with Down syndrome? He could be talking about our baby." I paused for a moment. "They are just retarded enough to know they're stupid," I mumbled while shaking my head in disbelief and complete disgust.

Gene looked at me. "I know he said some awful things, but it is scary, isn't it? Do you think you should have the amnio?"

"No, Gene. I'm not having an abortion even if there is something wrong."

"I know that, but wouldn't you want to be prepared?" Gene asked.

"Amnios are pretty risky. Do you want to take the chance of losing another baby?"

Gene looked at me, surprised I could ask such a question. I was surprised at myself. "Of course not," he said, "I just… never mind. I'm sorry I suggested it."

I took Gene's hand in mine. "I know; it scares me too, but we have to trust. Just because I'm 39 doesn't mean there's going to be something wrong. Look at my mom; she had me when she was forty-one and Chrissie when she was forty-four. Let's not worry about it."

"Do you want to go back to that genius?" Gene asked with sarcasm.

"I'll search out other options, don't worry."

I squeezed Gene's hand. "It will be fine."

Chapter Sixteen

The smell of my homemade spaghetti sauce filled the air in the kitchen, while the sound of the crackling fireplace came from the next room. The den was the coziest room in our house. It was originally a simple breezeway. The room connected the house to the garage. When we bought the home the fireplace was there, but it was dark brick and lined the entire wall. I was elated to have a fireplace, but knew we would eventually change the face of it and also get rid of the brick wall, which we did. Gene did an amazing job building the frame and mantel for it. It was painted white. The floor was covered in a beige Berber carpet, its walls were red, and complemented the white dental crown molding and Victorian furniture quite nicely. There were two walls of slotted windows, which Gene insisted on changing to narrow double hung windows, placed only a couple of inches apart. French-style atrium doors led out to our deck, which overlooked an inviting in-ground pool. We had done so much to the house, and we were both very pleased with the semi-final outcome.

"We have forty-five minutes until we have to leave," I said, as I pushed myself away from the table covered with the remainder of the dinner I had made; meatballs, sauce, pasta, Italian bread, and salad. I ate some plain pasta and some bread, but my stomach couldn't take much more.

"Paul, can you help me clear the table? Grace, your skirt and blouse are hanging on your doorknob. If you need help with your hair, let me know." I slowly got up from my chair.

"Do you know where my stockings are?" Grace asked as she stopped halfway up the stairs.

"Oh, yeah, they are on the foot of your bed. Do your best to move quickly, Grace, I want to get good seats," I said as I carried the plates to the sink.

"Good seats?" Paul asked sarcastically. "It's a puny elementary school auditorium, not a coliseum."

"Why are you speaking that way to your mother?" Gene asked as he helped clean the table.

"It's okay. Go ahead and laugh, Paul. I just want to be close enough to your sister's pretty face while she's singing."

"Pretty face?"

"Enough, Paul, go upstairs now and get ready," Gene said with a hint of anger.

"Oh, come on, I'm only kidding. But do I really have to go to this thing?" Paul whined.

"Of course you do. There isn't a single school concert of yours that she has missed. Besides, you need to start feeling a little bit of that Christmas spirit."

"I don't think hearing a bunch of fourth and fifth graders singing "Rudolf the Red Nose Reindeer" is going to do it for me, Ma."

"Never mind, go upstairs and get ready," Gene blurted out again.

"Yeah, okay," Paul said with a typical teenage attitude.

ॐॐ

The night air was bitter cold. As we walked through the school parking lot I could feel the wind cut through me like ice. It seemed now that I was pregnant, that I felt everything to the extreme. Although the main corridor of the school was as crowded as a New York City subway during rush hour, the warmth of it felt great me. There was no need to walk ourselves to the auditorium/cafeteria, the swarms of proud parents and family all naturally gravitated in that direction, as if someone was standing there in its doorway holding a huge magnet and we were being unwillingly pulled in. Once inside, I was overwhelmed by the scent of perfume coming from all the women that were around me. There was also a hint of stale food in the air, which I am sure was from the day's lunch served eight hours before. I covered my mouth and nose in order not to gag, which I knew would probably have to be the case for the rest of the evening, with the exception of having to pull my hand away from my face to clap for the children.

One by one the fourth graders walked into the auditorium. Some of them were giggling. Several walked with their heads down, while others had major looks of fear on their faces. All of them were adorable.

There she was, our Gracie, standing beside her good friend Shannon. Both of them were smiling, standing proudly on the third bleacher. Shannon elbowed Gracie, and then pointed at Gene, Paul and me. Gracie eyeballed the audience and spotted us. A look of pride took over her face, and she began to wave almost frantically. We waved back with the same amount of pride. I again thought about how blessed I was. These are the moments, I thought, what it's all about. One song after the other was performed by the little cuties. "Dradle Dradle", "Rudolf the Red Nosed Reindeer", "Silent night." It wasn't until their rendition of "Jingle Bell Rock" did I notice a little boy in the audience several rows in front of us bopping in perfect time to the music. I saw him from the back. He appeared to be the size of a three or four-year old, and he had very dark hair, cut in a surfer style. He wore khaki pants and a navy blue sweater. It was hard to take my eyes off of him. I was enjoying watching Gracie, but would glance at him every few seconds. Finally, he turned around, and that's when I saw his precious face. He had tan skin, full lips, a tiny button nose, and dark Mongolian eyes.

"Oh my goodness, he has Down syndrome," I said to myself.

"Gene, look at him, look at that little boy."

"Where?" he asked.

"He's in the fourth row, the one dancing, with the dark hair. Look at him go, he has so much music in him, and he has Down syndrome."

Gene spotted him and smiled. "Aw, he's so cute."

The song ended and the children took a bow. The audience got to their feet, and applause and whistles filled the room. Gracie looked at us for approval, and I'm sure she saw in our faces how proud we were. We watched as they all stepped off of the bleachers and exited the room in a very orderly fashion.

The principal, Mrs. Halpert, approached the microphone. "Thank you so much for attending tonight's concert. I'm sure you all agree that our music teacher Miss Dunn did a wonderful job with the children." Again the audience broke into applause. "There will be refreshments served in the main corridor. Have a wonderful holiday, everyone."

Everyone was moving around me, but my eyes were fixed on that little boy. I pushed my way past Gene, Paul, and the others. I had to follow him. I reached the door and searched for him, but he was already gone.

"Beautiful job, Gracie," Gene practically whispered as Grace hugged him goodnight.

"Yeah, not bad, Gracie," Paul admitted. Grace was beaming, especially from hearing that from her big brother.

"Thanks, Daddy. Thanks, Paul."

"She always does a great job," I boasted.

"And she's always the prettiest one there," Gene said as he kissed Gracie on top of the head.

"Good night kids. It's late, upstairs now. I'll be up in a minute," I said. Paul and Grace slowly walked up the stairs. "No TV." I shouted up at them, "and say your prayers." As that cold December day came to a close, and I lay in my warm comfortable bed, I reflected on the day and evening's events, feeling particularly full and blessed.

ॐ

I woke up the next day feeling happy about the prior evening and also that it was Friday. For some reason I always felt more energized on a Friday, probably because I knew Gene would be home both Saturday and Sunday. As sick as I sometimes would get being pregnant, I didn't venture out too often; it was hard for me to drive that way. On the weekends Gene would be my chauffeur. He would run my errands with me, and now that it was Christmas time, he would Christmas shop with me. Gene was so good about things like that, and he never complained about it. This particular day I did have to go out, though. We were going to our friends' Terri and Frank's for dinner, and to exchange gifts. Kelly and Larry would be joining us as well.

We had decided we would do a Kris Kringle. Two weeks before we had gotten together, we put our names in a hat and each picked out a name. Who you picked was to be kept a secret until the night of the dinner; we couldn't even tell our spouses who we had. As it turned out, I picked Larry, and couldn't get any advice from either Gene or Kelly on what to buy him. Today would be the day I had to buy something. I was always a last-minute shopper.

Both children went off to school, and Gene to work. I took a shower and painted my pale face with makeup, trying desperately to cover the dark circles under my eyes. I wasn't very successful. Oh, well. I went to pick out something to wear, not very successful in that department either. I felt like my clothes were already getting tight. I don't know if it was my imagination, or if it was because it was my fifth pregnancy, and my stomach muscles weren't what they used to be. That must be it. I decided on a pair of jeans and an oversized button-down denim shirt that belonged to Gene. It wasn't very attractive, but it was comfortable. I collected my pocketbook, keys, and a bottle of water, and headed out the door right as the phone rang.

"Hello?"

"Hi Jane, it's Jane Curtin."

"Oh, hey, Jane, how are you?"

"I'm good, I'm calling to see how you're feeling."

"I'm doing okay, Jane, you know how I get. I'm getting so frustrated because there is so much to do with the holidays approaching and I have so little ambition, and I'm constantly on the verge of throwing up. I don't know how my family is putting up with me."

"You are just like your mom."

My poor mom, she got sick the first five months of all ten pregnancies (She lost one at five months pregnant). She was that sick, and had two children in diapers all of the time – cloth diapers. I don't know how she did it. My kids were in school all day, and I was lucky if I got all of the beds made, did the dishes, and ran the vacuum. What a wimp!

"I wish I was. She had a lot more stamina than I do."

"Hon, I'm also calling to let you know I have a last minute job coming up. It's a big one. It starts on Monday as a prep day, and will go through Friday. I wanted to give you the opportunity to take the job before I called someone else."

Immediately my stomach went into knots. I wanted to take the job because I wanted Jane to be able to count on me, no matter what, and we could've really used the money. The problem was not Monday, the prep day. That would be an eight-hour day, consisting of basic tasks like cutting vegetables, sorting cheese, and making dough. It was the rest of the week that would be killer. Those days we would probably work upwards of 15-hour days, and with the smell of the pizza sauce, I really didn't think I could do it.

"Oh, Jane, I want to do it in the worst way, but honestly, I don't want you to hire me and then me conk out on you halfway through the job. I also don't want to be running to the bathroom every half an hour from the smell of the sauce. It wouldn't be fair to you or the other girls."

"Oh, I understand completely, just thought I'd ask."

"I'm sorry, Jane."

"No problem. So how are Paul and Grace?"

"We're all doing fine, thanks."

"Have you seen the doctor yet?"

"Oh, have I." I proceeded to tell her the horror story of mine and Gene's conversation with my ever lovin' doctor. Naturally, she was appalled.

"That is absolutely barbaric," she said, disgusted. "He shouldn't even be practicing medicine; I certainly hope you're switching doctors."

"I know I have to, but I've been putting it off. You know how I'm a procrastinator, and it's going to be difficult to do. I'm supposed stay with the same doctor in our group."

"It doesn't matter if it's going to be difficult, you can't go to him, Jane. I'm sure many women have switched doctors, and they probably won't give you a hard time. With the way this guy sounds, I'm sure it's not the first complaint they've gotten about him. Do you really want this, whatever you want to call him, to help you bring your baby into this world?"

"I know. You're right," I sighed.

I so often listened to her advice, and so often she was right. I just hated any sort of confrontation with anyone. I knew it was time for me to make some phone calls, but decided I'd give myself the weekend. I'd make the calls Monday.

"I promise the next time we speak, it will all be worked out."

"I don't want to tell you what to do Jane, but I know you. You can't go through the next seven months of prenatal care with that you-know-what."

"I know, I know. I'll let you know when I get another appointment," I said, feeling grateful she cared so much. I knew she was right.

"Bye, sweetheart, talk to you soon."

"Bye, Jane. Thanks for thinking of me."

I hung up the phone, grabbed my belongings once again, and went out the door. I couldn't help but feel defeated. It wasn't about the doctor, it was more about losing the job, but I knew I couldn't be all I should be if I was there. It was the right thing to do all around.

I did go shopping for Larry. I decided after much deliberation that I should get him a mustache trimmer and comb (as a joke of course), and some nice cigars. Our guys loved cigars. I stopped on the main highway at the Smoke Shop and trusted the owner's opinion on selecting a few.

❦

"I'll be out in the car," Gene shouted, "warming it up."

"Okay, hon. Give me five minutes," I said, fussing with my hair. Looking into the mirror, I saw in its reflection how tired I looked, and how especially pale. "Ugh, I look awful," I mumbled to myself.

I walked upstairs and into Paul's room. "Be nice to your sister while we're gone, we want no bad reports when we get home. Terri and Frank's number is on the island. Call us if you need us."

"Yeah, okay, mom," Paul said.

"There are plenty of snacks for you guys."

"Thanks, Mrs. Spiotta," Lawrence said. Lawrence was a close friend of Paul's that used to stay with us on weekends after his family moved away. We had grown to love him like our own. Paul appeared to be a bit annoyed because they were in the middle of playing a Play Station game.

"Gotcha, Mom. Thanks."

"Gracie is downstairs with Shannon. Remember, no teasing."

"Okay, okay. Good night, mom."

"Good night, boys."

I quickly walked downstairs to find the girls dancing to

Aretha Franklin's "Respect". They were so darn cute; I could have stood there watching them all night.

"Girls, the boys are upstairs. You know where Terri's number is. Please call us if you need anything. Make sure you lock the doors, and don't answer the door for anyone." I couldn't help but think of how Gene was sitting in the car, not worried about a thing, I had it all covered. I was obviously was the annoying parent, and that was okay by me. I knew someday my kids would get it.

Gracie ran towards me. "Goodnight, mom," she said as she put her thumb on my belly and blessed it… again. I kissed her and rubbed the top of her head. "Good night, honey." I waved to Shannon, who smiled and waved back.

Gracie followed me. "I'll lock the door behind you."

"Thanks, sweetie. Be good." Gracie rolled her eyes. Somehow I always had to have the last word.

I looked at Gene as we drove up to Terri and Frank's house. "Oh, no, I forgot the gifts."

"I took them. They're in the back seat."

I looked at him in earnest. "Did you bring the dip and chips?"

"Right next to the gifts," he said matter-of-factly.

"I'm sorry, hon. I feel especially forgetful the last few weeks."

"I guess I can cut you some slack, but you owe me."

"I owe you?" I said as I tapped his hand. "Yeah, we'll see, we'll see," I giggled. "Remember, I'm the one carrying your precious child sick as a dog. I'd say we're even."

Gene smiled at me. "Come on. Let's go in." He walked around the car to open my door to help me out, typical for him, always polite. As we stepped out into the street, we saw Kelly and Larry pull up. Larry parked his shiny black Dodge ram pickup truck. He stepped out of the truck and walked around to help Kelly out, as Gene did me. We walked toward them, shivering from the cold air, and greeted one another as we always did.

"Hey, guys. Are you ready for some secret Santa?" Larry said as he squeezed me.

"You know it," Gene said loudly.

"Hey, Kel, How are you feeling?" I asked.

"Good, good, no complaints. How about you, are you still sick to your stomach?"

"Yeah, unfortunately it's par for the course with me. It seems to be easing a little, though."

Larry looked at all of us. "I can tell you how I feel. Cold," he said through chattering teeth. "Let's go inside."

As we walked up to the house, Frank appeared behind the semi-frosted glass door with a big smile. Frank couldn't give a small smile, his grin always traveled from ear to ear and showed off his sparkling white teeth. He was tall, with jet-black hair, which made our nickname for him not unsuitable. We would call him, Ponch, From the T.V. show Chips, or Donny of the Osmond variety.

"Welcome folks, come on in."

We all stepped into the foyer. Their house was a split ranch, so we all climbed the four steps up to the main level of their home. Their Christmas decorations were displayed beautifully. An artificial tree (that looked surprisingly real) stood in the corner of the living room. It wore flashing white lights and very contemporary ornaments — quite pretty. The nativity set was arranged under the large bay window, and was modern looking as well. I personally prefer more traditional looking decorations, but I could certainly appreciate Terri and Frank's taste. Terri was standing in the dining room putting the last of the silverware on the lovely set table. Lit candles were placed throughout, which were very noticeable because of the dim lights.

Terri smiled. "Hello, there, welcome everyone," she said in her sweet soft voice. Her voice matched her face, sweet and soft. She had big green eyes, a perfect little nose, and a fair, beautiful complexion. She too, had dark hair, which she often wore up in twist. What a lady she was. Terri walked over to us and we all exchanged greetings. Frank took the dip and chips from Gene and a tray of shrimp cocktail from Larry.

"Have a seat," Terri said as she took our coats "Would you like something to drink?"

"Nothing for me yet, thanks," I said as I put our gifts under the tree.

Kelly followed behind me. "I'll have some ice water," she said as Larry and Gene followed Frank into the kitchen and helped themselves to a beer. All of us were finally gathered around the coffee table, which was filled with delicious hors d'oeuvres.

As we munched away, Terri turned to me. "So how are you girls doing? Did you go to the doctor yet, Jane?"

"I sure did," I said, rolling my eyes. "What a nightmare."

Gene looked at me and then at the rest of them. "Wait till you hear this one!" I proceeded to share with them the horrific experience that took place at my doctor's visit. They all looked at us with disbelief, shaking their heads.

Kelly looked the most disturbed and puzzled. "That is so strange. There's a girl I work with that's pregnant, she told me a similar story a couple of weeks ago."

"Really?" I asked with a great deal of surprise. "Who is her doctor?"

"I don't know, but I do know that she belonged to an H.M.O. I referred her to my group of doctors. Apparently they let her go outside the center without switching her other doctors. They didn't give her a hard time. Her doctor had to be the same doctor as yours. There couldn't be two doctors like him."

I was so relieved to hear what I had heard. "You have no idea what news that is for us. I have to get your doctor's name and number before I leave tonight. I'll be calling first thing Monday morning."

Then Larry chimed in. "Odd that you should bring up Down syndrome. Today when I was at work, this guy Mike ran out of the office crying. His wife had just called to tell him that their amnio results came back, and that their baby had Down syndrome."

All of us looked over at him with sadness on our faces. "That must have been devastating for them to hear," Terri said with a scowl.

Frank cleared his throat to change the subject. "What do you say we exchange gifts now?"

"Great idea," Gene said.

Larry laughed at the mustache trimmer and comb, and

seemed very pleased with the cigars. Frank had picked me. He gave me a cinnamon scented candle, which smelled delicious, along with a CD called "Time in a Bottle" that held a collection of songs from our era. I loved the gifts, but what was so special about it was how evident it was that we knew each other so well. Everyone's gift suited them perfectly. We finished opening gifts and then sat down at the dining room table to an extravagant five-course dinner. I remember as we sat and ate, hearing the buzz of everyone's voices, and also muddled laughter. I was completely zoned out through the entire meal. All I kept thinking was, Okay, God, what are you trying to tell me?

Chapter Seventeen

Monday morning arrived and I called the H.M.O group I belonged to, to inquire about switching doctors. Kelly was right, there was no problem. Not a single question was asked. After, I called Kelly's group of doctors.

"Southside Medical Group, can I help you?"

"Yes, I was referred to you by my friend Kelly Smith, who is a patient in your office. I was a patient over at an H.M.O center and was displeased with my doctor. I understand you accept my insurance and I was wondering if you're willing to take me on as a patient."

"That shouldn't be a problem," the women replied, "I'll have to get some information from you."

"Sure. I do have to tell you that I am expecting a baby in July."

"Oh. Congratulations. We'll have to get you in here fairly soon, then. I believe the earliest appointment is the first week in January, January 4th to be exact, 9 a.m. Does that work for you?"

"That sounds great to me."

"Okay, then. You're scheduled for the 4th at 9 o'clock with Dr. Johnson. If you experience any problems, just give us a call and we'll fit you in."

"Thank you for your help."

I gave her all of the information required, and that was that. I was so relieved and grateful that I didn't have to return to that you-know-what. Now I'd be able to concentrate on Christmas. It was approaching quickly. There was much to do. It was tradition that some of my family would come and stay for a few days before and through Christmas. Of course, my beloved parents would drive 600 miles from Southern N.J., while my sister Tess, my brother in-law Bob, their three children, my sister Chrissie, and brother-in-law Billy and their two children would drive from other areas of down south as well. Kathy lived in the apartment adjacent to our house, so thankfully she was with us, too. Sadly, Grace wasn't with us, the only sister missing. We felt her absence, all the more at

Christmas, and yet we knew her spirit was there. Our brothers were with their wives' families. Although we missed them, we understood that was where they should be.

It was three days before Christmas. I was completely exhausted from all of the shopping for gifts and for food, never mind the last minute cleaning and decorating that had to be done. Our tree was the last thing to be decorated. We waited for the family to arrive to do that. It was yet another tradition. It was one I thoroughly enjoyed; we all did. I would put the Amy Grant Christmas CD in the CD player, and we'd watch Paul, Gracie, Ryan, Sean, Kathleen, Jamie and Shannon decorate it. Ryan, Sean, and Kathleen were Tess and Bob's children. Jamie and Shannon were Chrissie and Billy's girls. All of them delightful, and close in age to Paul and Gracie. They loved being together. It was always evident in their faces. Being in the midst of their excitement was always magical to witness.

Anyway, back to that night. I don't know why it sticks out in my mind, it just does. I was at my kitchen island wrapping last minute gifts. I had chicken cutlets and potatoes baking in the oven. Paul, recently becoming a vegetarian, didn't want the chicken. He decided to microwave a veggie burger. In the meantime, Gene was taking a shower. When he finished, he opened the bathroom door, wafting the pungent fragrance of Irish Spring soap from the bathroom into the kitchen. At the same time, Paul opened the microwave oven door to expose the smell of his cooked veggie burger. The combination of those two scents was enough to throw me over the edge. I will never forget it. I hastily walked down to our musty smelling basement to stop myself from vomiting. I stayed down there until the air cleared, which was a good part of the evening. I even had Gene bring my dinner down to me. I sat on an old couch we had down there, crying, so sick of feeling sick, wondering when it would go away for good. I must mention that that particular night was also the first night of many, many nights that I woke up with severe pains in my thighs. It felt like someone was stabbing me in the legs. It was awful.

❧◈❧

It was Christmas Eve, and by then everyone that was coming to visit had arrived. All of the children were excited (as always), and so were us parents. There is something about Christmas that brings out the child in most of us, in a good way. My mother, sisters, our girls, and I spent the afternoon baking, while the men watched a movie in the den. Then it was time to think about Mass. We all decided to go to the evening Mass, while Gene opted to stay home and prepare dinner for us (what a guy!).The Christmas celebration was beautiful but packed. We managed to find two seats for our parents. The rest of us stood through the service.

We arrived back home and walked into bliss. Gene had Christmas music playing. The fireplace was crackling, the table was set, and a candelabra with its lit candles illuminated the table beautifully. Gene took care of all of it. Sometimes I wondered how I wound up with Gene. Although he loved to be busy and constantly be doing something, it wasn't just about that. He really gave all of his time and energy with his heart.

"Hey, how was church?"

"We were packed in like sardines," Dad said. Mom thought it was a lovely Mass, of course.

Dad hung up his coat, walked over to the counter to make his martini, and then poured a glass of wine for my mother. Tess, Chrissie, and Kathy joined my mother in a glass of wine. I couldn't.

"Gene, the place looks wonderful," my dad said. We all agreed.

"Can I do something, hon?"

"No, it's all taken care of."

Kathy went next to Gene, gave him a hug, teasing him, "You're the best, Geno." Gene then placed a huge platter of scallops wrapped in bacon on the center of the island. We devoured them as if we hadn't eaten in days. I remember thinking as I was eating them how amazing it was that I could eat something as rich as scallops in bacon, yet I couldn't handle the smell of a veggie burger.

There was only one left when my niece Jamie asked, "How about we raffle it off?"

"Good idea," Grace replied.

Knowing her grandpa wouldn't eat more than two, nor would my mother (for health reasons only, she certainly loved her food, and would be the first to admit it.), Gracie said, "Grandpa, you think of a number in your head and whisper it to Grandma." We were all giggling. Then each of us guessed a number. Guess who won? Me. I immediately saw the disappointment in Jamie's face, so I gave it to her. It sounds so silly, the whole idea of it, but they were really delicious. We still laugh about it to this day.

Everyone enjoyed a delicious meal of shrimp, garlic, and fresh spinach over pasta, filet mignon, tossed salad, and Italian bread. I stuck to just the bread and salad as the shrimp was too much for me. All were compliments of Gene—he was quite the cook. The evening continued with lots of laughter, good conversation, and was followed by singing Christmas carols around the piano, which my mother's talented hands and ear graced us with. The children happily went off to bed, while we mothers stuffed our children's stockings. The fathers assembled what needed to be assembled and placed all the gifts under the tree. Mom and Dad stood by watching, I'm sure remembering in their mind and hearts doing the same for all of us. How bittersweet.

Morning came quickly as the alarm went off at 5:30 a.m. Another tradition of ours was to wake early to open gifts. There were many to open, and there was a lot of prepping to do. We were having at least 30 people for dinner that day.

"Gene, wake up. We have to get everyone up. There are presents to open, breakfast to make and a turkey to get in the oven." The poor guy, I could be such a nag. I'd like to blame it on the hormones or pregnancy, but it wouldn't be right. I could be a nag at any given time, pregnant or not. Thank God Gene was so good-natured.

"Calm down, hon, and Merry Christmas," he said joyfully as he kissed me on the cheek. He jumped up, put his robe on, and quickly left the room, surely to turn the Christmas tree lights on. After washing up and brushing my teeth, I went into the kitchen to put the coffee on. Gene lit a fire in the fireplace; I went to wake my sisters and parents.

Our children stood at the top of the stairs as the dads prepared their cameras. "You can come down, now."

All seven of them raced down the stairs. Their eyes opened wide at the amount of gifts that they saw. Looking back, it was a little ridiculous. Gene and I were the worst culprits in spoiling our children at Christmas. It literally took us two hours to open gifts, but it was a fun morning. We cleaned up the wrapping paper and put most of the gifts away as best we could. After that we started to prepare for our afternoon guests. Gene's Mom and her fiancé Kenny, my sister in-law Mary, Frank, Gene's Aunt Mary, Uncle Gary and his Aunt T, his cousin David and Kathy's friend Jerry joined us, too. It was a large crowd to cook for but with the help of my sisters, we pulled it off. Our guests enjoyed a meal of roast turkey, stuffing, mashed potatoes, green bean casserole, and stuffed shells made by my mother-in-law. All in all, it was a beautiful Christmas, but needless to say, by the end of it I was exhausted. After everyone was done, all of us sat in my den and watched "The Sound of Music". Our favorite part was watching my father's face when Christopher Plumber sang "Edelweiss", it was his favorite. A perfect ending to a nearly perfect day.

The next few days were fun just because we were together. We didn't do much; returned some gifts, had lunch, and then we all went for a pedicure together. Sisterly things to do, which we didn't often have the pleasure of doing. My cousin Janie came to stay with us for a few days. She was Gracie, Kathleen, and Shannon's age. They all got along famously. They wrote a little play, "A modern Cinderella." They performed it for us. They were adorable. Whenever they were together they would always put on a show for us. We did the same thing when we were kids. Such fun. Soon it was time for everyone to go home. I hated that part, it was always so hard to say goodbye. Mom and Dad would stay with us for another week or two. We shared our tearful goodbyes and they were on their way.

"I'll be going to the doctor next week. I'm sure they'll give me a sonogram. I'll send you guys a picture," I yelled as they were getting into their cars. My mom, dad, Gracie and I stood at the door waving. Ouch—that always hurt.

Chapter Eighteen

Gene and I left for the doctor's by 8:15. It was only a ten-minute ride, but I figured I'd have to fill out some paperwork, seeing as how it was my first visit to that office. It turned out that I was right. There was a lot of paperwork to fill out. I had just about finished it when I was called into the examining room. A petite brunette woman wearing bright pink scrubs escorted me and Gene to the room. She proceeded to weigh me and jot down my weight. 136 – I had only gained two pounds. I wasn't surprised, I only had an occasional appetite. She then handed me a little plastic cup.

"I'm going to need a sample, just leave it in the bathroom when you're done. Dr. Johnson will be with you shortly."

"Okay. Thanks. No gown, no exam today?" I asked her, puzzled.

"Not this visit. This is just a consultation, an exam really isn't necessary."

"Okay," I said. I was actually quite happy I didn't have to have one. All of us women know it isn't a very pleasant experience.

Gene sat in the chair while I sat on the edge of the examining table. Dr. Johnson came in. He was a tall man, with blonde curly hair.

"Hello, there." He shook both of our hands. "I'm Dr. Johnson," he said, smiling.

"Nice to meet you," we both replied.

"So it says here that you're expecting in July," he said as he listened to my heart. "Just lay back, I want to measure your belly and listen to the baby's heartbeat."

He went on to measure my belly, then put the stethoscope on my stomach. "Wow, that's cold!" I said, jumping slightly.

"Oh, sorry," he said. That was when we heard the sound of the baby's heartbeat. What an incredible thrill. Gene and I were beaming. "Well, that's a good strong heartbeat. How are you feeling?" he asked as he took the stethoscope from his ears.

"Well, I don't have the best appetite, which is typical

for me during pregnancy, so it doesn't concern me. I have, however, been waking up in the middle of the night with terrible pain in my thighs. I never felt anything like it before. It feels like I'm being stabbed."

"That's interesting; I've never heard that complaint before. Not sure that's related to your pregnancy. How old are you, Jane?"

"39."

"You know, you're at a higher risk of having problems with your pregnancy and with your baby because of your age. We consider over 35 being high risk. You might want to consider having an amniocentesis.

"No, Doctor, we don't want to do that. We wouldn't do anything anyway.

"Okay. I can respect that. I'd like you to have a sonogram though, just to make sure you're correct with your dates. There's a sono tech here today. I'll set that up for you right now. As far as the pain in your legs, there is no harm in taking Tylenol for that. If it continues, let me know and we'll have to look into it further. In the meantime, you can go back to the waiting room where it's more comfortable. It shouldn't be too long of a wait for the sonogram."

"Thanks, Doctor," Gene said as he stood up to shake the doctor's hand.

"Yes, thanks, Doctor," I said.

"No problem. Make an appointment for four weeks from now. Be sure to take your vitamins. I'll leave a script with the receptionist for some routine blood work that needs to be done. Have a good day, folks," he said as he walked out the door.

"You, too," we both said. We were both so happy. What a difference between the first doctor and Dr. Johnson.

We didn't have to wait long to be called in. The sonogram room was very small; it barely had room for the examining table and large machine that stood next to it. The sono technician introduced herself as Ellen, and although she seemed pleasant enough by smiling a lot, she didn't have much to say. I changed into the gown she gave me in a tiny bathroom that was adjacent to the examining room. I lay down on the table. She opened the gown to expose my belly and began to squeeze a clear gel onto my abdomen. "This will be a little cold," she warned.

Gene and I joined her in looking up at a little TV screen that was attached to the machine. She glided the wand across my stomach, while pushing down at the same time. It was a little uncomfortable.

"There's the heart." We were overjoyed to watch it beating.

"Can you tell what it is? Not that we want to know. Oh Gene, look at the baby move," I said. I was so excited.

"No, I can't tell yet," she said as she slid the wand around. That's when I noticed her face go from smiling to stone cold. She then typed something into the machine, and printed out some photos for us.

"Okay. You can go get dressed now."

"That's it?"

"Yes, for now, that's it." She said it so abruptly. "The doctor will call you in to his office to talk to you. You can wait in the waiting room."

"Okay. I'll meet you out there Gene, or do you want to wait for me to get dressed?"

"I'll wait, babe."

I went into the bathroom feeling a little strange about what had just transpired. I thought we were through with the doctor today. I quickly wiped the gel off of my stomach, got dressed, washed my hands, and walked back into the examining room. Gene was standing there with an odd look on his face.

"Okay. What's wrong?" I asked him, panicking.

"She said she saw something on the baby's head, but it could be nothing."

"What do you mean!?" I cried, confused.

"She said the doctor would talk to us, so we'll have to hear what he has to say."

I stood there shaking like a leaf. I leaned onto the examining table, weak from fear. Gene took hold of me and put his arm around me to help me walk out of the office and into the waiting room. As we were walking down the corridor, the sono tech approached us. "I feel so bad," she said, "the doctor left the office. Why don't you go home? When one of our doctors here reads the sonogram, they'll call you. It shouldn't be more than an hour."

"What did you see?" I whined.

"I can tell you that I did see a little something on the baby's head, but that's all I can tell you. I understand you're nervous, but I think your best bet is to go home and wait for one of our doctors to call you."

The only thing I remember after that was being in the car with Gene, driving down the main highway. I was crying hysterically. "How are we going to tell the kids? This is a nightmare." I continued to cry, while Gene drove in silence, holding the steering wheel with one hand and holding my hand with the other, stroking the top of my hand with his thumb in an effort to sooth me. We arrived home, and Gene walked me into the house. My dad was standing by the kitchen sink. He turned around to us when he heard us walk in.

"Hi, how did it go?"

I could tell when he looked at me that he knew there was something wrong. He immediately walked over to me.

"What's wrong?"

I fell into his arms, weeping. "Dad, there's something wrong with the baby." I was sobbing with my head on his shoulder. I cried even harder as he wrapped his arms around me.

"Oh, no," he said softly. "It'll be okay, honey. What did the doctor say, Gene?"

Gene took a big breath and let it out slowly. "Well, we didn't even speak to a doctor yet. The sonogram technician said she saw something on the baby's head. The doctor should be calling here soon."

"Come on Jane, sit down," my dad said as he walked me over to the couch. My mom was sitting there, and began rubbing my back as soon as I sat down.

"Jane dear, don't panic, wait to hear what the doctor has to say."

"Mom, what am I going to tell the kids? They're so excited about this baby, they're gonna be heartbroken."

"Like your mom said, let's wait and hear from the doctor."
Gene tried to be optimistic, but I knew he was scared, too.

After a very long half-hour the phone rang. "Hello, Mrs.
Spiotta, this is Dr. Klein," a woman's voice said. "I'm sorry
there wasn't a doctor to speak to you when you were here. I
looked over your results. Your baby has something on the back
of its head. It's called a cystic hygroma."

"What's that?" I felt my body beginning to weaken once
again. I must have had some expression on my face, because
Gene immediately brought a chair over to me, made me sit,
then took the phone and put it on speaker.

"It's a fluid-filled sac that occurs when there is a
blockage in the lymphatic system. It's associated with a few
chromosome disorders. It also could be nothing and dissolve
itself. One other scenario is that your baby is perfectly normal,
with the exception of the hygroma, and if it doesn't dissolve,
would have to be surgically removed after he or she is born.
Either way, I would like you to see a genetic counselor right
away. I'm going to transfer you to our receptionist Lisa, and
she'll set up an appointment for you."

"Okay," we both answered, not able to say anything else.

"Hello, Jane?"

"Yes, this is she," I replied with a shaky voice while Gene
and my parents listened in.

"Hi, honey, I have County General Hospital on the line.
One of their genetic counselors has an available spot for 11
a.m. tomorrow. Will that work for you?" I looked at Gene, and
he nodded in agreement.

"Yes, that would be fine."

"Her name is Susan Harrison. When you get to the
hospital, go through the main doors. There will be an
information booth to your right. Someone there will direct you
to Susan's office. Good luck to you, Jane."

"Thank you so much," I said before I hung up the phone.
We all stood there dumbfounded. There was nothing to say.
My dad broke the silence.

"I bet it's nothing. Look at your mother, she had nine
healthy pregnancies. There's no history of anything going
wrong with any of our family." My poor dad, he meant well,

he was just trying to make us feel better, and part of me believes that he really believed it, too.

Gene began to walk away. He was visibly upset. "I'm going to call my mother." Unbeknownst to me, he asked his mother to come with us to the genetic counselor in his conversation with her. I was glad that she was coming.

Gene and I spent the remainder of the afternoon making phone calls. We let my siblings know. Gene's sister, too. We called our close friends as well. We needed all of the prayers we could get. We finished up before the children got home from school, and then we put on our happy faces for them. We decided it was best not to tell them until we knew what it was that we were facing. No need to worry them yet.

It was a long night for most of us. I didn't get any sleep, not just because of the news of our baby, but the pains in my legs were atrocious. I finally rolled out of bed at 6 a.m. I prepared the table for breakfast, then sat and waited for everyone to wake up, which was only about a half-hour's wait. I sat there worrying about our baby and what Paul's and Gracie's reaction would be to what may be wrong. Hearing my dad walk into the kitchen snapped me out of it. I didn't have to look up to see who it was. I knew the sound of his footsteps.

"Good morning, Jane." He walked over to me and touched my cheek with his large strong hand, a true sign of affection from him. "How did you sleep, honey?"

"Not very well."

"I didn't, either. I feel so terrible for you and Gene," he said in a compassionate tone before he sat across from me.

"I know, Dad, truthfully, I feel bad for us too. I especially feel bad for the kids." I changed the subject. I didn't want to start crying again. "How did Mom sleep?"

"You know how she sleeps. She isn't feeling this as hard as she would have before she had the stroke. I guess that's a good thing in a way."

"She gets it, Dad, I think she's just praying and giving it away."

"She's still not completely the same."

I nodded in agreement.

∂∾ớ

The children were finally up, and it was all I could do to maintain some degree of composure or calmness around them. Every time I looked at Gracie I had to keep myself from crying. I had to dismiss the thought of the baby around both of the children in order to do that.

Paul and Grace left for school. Dad helped me clean up breakfast, while mom sat on the couch and clipped coupons. Mom at that point was quite feeble, and was not very steady on her feet. Otherwise she would have been up helping me. She had always been eager to help with everything; she was so full of life and energy. She was slowly declining, and it was hard to watch. I was grateful that as feeble as she was, she still had managed to play piano—it kept her going.

Dad, on the other hand, had the mind and energy of someone in his 60s. At the age of 89, he was still completely capable of driving."What time will you and Gene leave here, Jane?" Dad asked as he put a pile of dirty dishes in the sink.

"Well, it takes at least half an hour to get to the hospital. Then there's parking, you never know what that'll be like. I'd say we should leave around 10:00. What time is your mom coming, Gene?" I asked as he helped clear the table.

"She said she would be here by 9:30, so I'm guessing she will be here around 10:00." We both laughed. My mother-in-law had a habit of being a little more than fashionably late. "Perfect, I said, "I'm glad she's coming."

Marge arrived by 9:45. She came into the house in a very positive state. I'm sure she was sick inside, but wanted to be strong for us. She was always quick with a joke and wore a big smile. She did have her smile on, but there were no jokes that day. Marge was an attractive woman, with short blonde hair, pretty green eyes, and white teeth that looked like Chicklets. She loved her gold jewelry, and wore it proudly around her neck, wrists, fingers and ears. She always looked put together, and smelled good; she wore the finest of fragrances.

"Hello kids. Gert and Bill, how are you?" She walked over to my parents and kissed them hello, then came over to us and gave us a quick hug. It was quick, probably to avoid showing too much emotion.

"What do you say we take off?" Gene asked. I knew he wanted to leave. There was so much tension in the air, but it was no one's fault. We were all just so upset. No one spoke, I think mainly out of fear of saying the wrong thing. So, we proceeded to say our goodbyes and we were on our way.

We pulled up to the County Hospital. It resembled the hospital that Grace had both worked and died in. I must say I had almost the same sick feeling I did the night we first arrived to see Grace the day before her passing. They weren't the exact same feelings, but the fear was just as intense.

We followed the walkway to the revolving doors. As we entered, Gene walked right over to the information desk. I could see the gentleman behind it, directing Gene where to go. Marge was standing with me, holding on to my trembling hand. Gene led us to a door that read "Genetic Counseling".

"This is it," Gene said. He opened the door to a small waiting room and walked up to the reception desk. "My wife and I have an appointment with Susan Harrison. Our names are Gene and Jane Spiotta."

"Oh yes," the middle-aged woman replied. "She's on a phone conference right now, she should be done in a few moments, you can all have a seat in the meantime," Her voice was very pleasant.

"Sure, thank you," he said softly. Gene sat down next to me, not saying a word. He picked up a magazine from the coffee table that was in front of us and started to thumb through it. He probably didn't even see what was on the pages. His mom just sat there in silence. I joined her.

Ten minutes later we were called into Susan's office. We asked the receptionist if Marge could come in with us, and she assured us it was no problem. Susan introduced herself. She was a young girl, probably in her late twenties, but looked about 18. She was plainly dressed, had an Irish-looking face and curly brown hair. She offered us a seat. We all took one. Not really wanting to hear what she had to say, or fearing it, I sat in the corner of the room furthest away from her. As if that would have actually made a difference. Susan sat down at her desk with a sympathetic look on her face. Not good, I thought.

"I know you must be frightened right now, and you must

have many questions. I'm going to explain to you what the cystic hygroma is and how it may or may not affect your baby. Please feel free to interrupt me at any time with any questions you may have." She paused and took a deep breath. "Your baby has a cystic hygroma on the back of its head, which appears from the sonogram to be quite large. It's caused by a blockage in the lymphatic system."

"Is it a growth?" Gene asked.

"No, it's actually a fluid-filled sac commonly associated with different syndromes, such as Turners Syndrome, Trisomy 13, 18, and 21."

"But the doctor said it could be nothing and that it could possibly dissolve," Marge stated with a hopeful tone. I just sat there, sick and dumbfounded. I couldn't speak.

"That's true," Susan replied, "and that is our hope for the baby and for all of you. It's important however, that I inform you of what you may be facing."

"Go ahead, tell us," Gene said, not without hesitation.

"As I said, Trisomy 13 is a possibility. It's when the child receives duplicated information from chromosome 13. Some of the symptoms would be a cleft palate and lip, close-set eyes, or fused eyes.

"Wait," I interrupted, "what do you mean, fused eyes?"

"Well, fused eyes give the appearance of having one eye."

"Oh, God," I cried. Marge rubbed my back as I cried uncontrollably.

"I'm sorry, Jane," Susan said as she handed Marge a box of tissues. "I feel terrible telling you these things, but you need to know what the possibilities are."

"Go ahead," Gene insisted.

"With this syndrome, the baby could have low muscle tone, a small head, seizures, missing skin, skeletal malformations, and severe mental retardation. These babies generally have feeding complications, breathing abnormalities, heart complications, and will be deaf. Because of the severe malformations of the disorder, most babies affected will be stillborn, or die within the first few months of life."

At that point we were all crying. I was in such a state I could barely breathe. Gene and Marge both tried to keep their composure so they could listen.

"Go on," he said.

"Well," she said with a great deal of compassion, "the next possibility would be Trisomy 18, otherwise known as Edwards syndrome. The child receives duplicated information from chromosome 18. This syndrome is more common in girls. Symptoms include mental retardation, kidney complications, low birth weight, heart abnormalities, clenched hands, crossed legs, small head and jaw, and malformed chest." At that point I was rocking back and forth, something I did to help sooth myself, and was weeping like a baby. I couldn't even look up at her. She continued "Most babies with this disorder will die within the first few weeks of life, and those that live beyond will need extensive medical care." She took a breath. "Then there is also a chance the baby could have Trisomy 21, otherwise known as Down syndrome. The symptoms can be from mild to severe. They include physical and mental delays, heart complications, dementia, hearing loss, vision abnormalities, thyroid complications, and skeletal abnormalities. They can lead fairly healthy lives with the help of others."

"How much more of this is there to hear? What are we going to do, Gene?" I asked as I sniffled, continuing to rock back and forth. He didn't say a word, just stared at Susan, waiting for the rest of the dreadful, possible scenarios.

"Turners is another syndrome associated with the hygroma. It's caused by the complete or partial absence of one of the two X chromosomes, normally found in a female. The child is always a female. Physical characteristics could include webbed neck and or arms slightly turned out at the elbow. They are susceptible to heart, kidney, and thyroid problems. They are also short in stature, and lack ovarian development. Proper medical care should help them lead a full and productive life."

At that point I was in a completely different world. Although some of the syndromes were far worse than others, all of them sounded horrendous to me. In my mind there was no preference of what this child would be afflicted with; all were a no option for me. My poor baby, I thought, this simply can't be happening.

Susan went on, "Of course there's a chance the baby could be completely normal with the exception of the hygroma. If that's the case, there is a possibility it could slowly dissolve during pregnancy, or if not, it can be removed by surgery after the child is born."

"Okay," Gene asked as he took a deep breath, "what's next, where do we go from here?"

"That's up to you. You can go have an amnio to determine what it is you're dealing with, or you can do nothing and ride the pregnancy out. Of course, it's still early enough for a termination, if that's what you decide. My advice to you is to go have the amnio so you know exactly what you're facing."

I was in a terrible state, which was obvious to Susan. She looked directly at me. "I'd like to give our obstetric specialist a call. He deals with high-risk pregnancies. Maybe he can fit you in today. He should be able to give you a level 2 sonogram right in his office, which might show you more of what condition your baby's in. He's the one you can speak with about having an amnio."

She called his office. They were able to fit us in about three hours later. We took the appointment gratefully. "His name is Dr. Doyle. He's a wonderful doctor, very thorough, with a great bedside manner. I'm sure you'll feel really comfortable with him, and that he'll be a great help to you." She gave us the directions and sent us on our way.

We had a few hours to spare, so with Marge's suggestion we stopped at a diner for something to eat. I ate nothing, while Gene and Marge picked at their food like birds.

We arrived at the doctor's office and were immediately called in to speak with him. He was a young doctor, strikingly handsome, which I'm surprised I noticed in the state of mind I was in. He was extremely kind and personable.

We exchanged handshakes. "Hello, Mr. and Mrs. Spiotta. Susan faxed over your records to me. I know this must be so difficult for you. I'm going to do all I can to help you. First thing I'd like to do is a level 2 sonogram. Our sonogram technician will do that for you. I'll stay and explain everything I see as she does it. You can get changed, and Kathryn and I will be back in just a few minutes."

There I was, 15 minutes later, lying on another table. Kathryn squeezed the gel onto my stomach and started the exam. Dr. Doyle stood by watching. He pointed to the screen. "See, there is the hygroma. It is large. It extends from its head almost to the tailbone."

It looked exactly how they described it—a water-filled sack. Almost like a long water balloon, adhered to the baby's back. I just lay there weeping. I couldn't pull myself together, I felt ashamed but I just couldn't.

Kathryn then slid the wand to show the baby's heart. "There happens to be a little spot on the baby's heart. It doesn't necessarily mean there is something wrong with it, but it could be a marker, we'll have to keep an eye on that."

Then she went down to the kidneys. "A spot on both kidneys as well," he said. At that point I was sobbing so hard I don't know how they finished the exam. I don't remember the rest of the exam beyond that point. I was too much of a basket case.

Eventually, when they finished up, he told me to get dressed, and that he would be back in to speak to us. I did, and we waited.

"I have to be honest with you. Between the cystic hygroma and the markings on the baby's heart and kidneys, it does point to some type of syndrome. There is, however, a slight chance that the baby is okay. I do feel bad for you folks. I see how deeply upset you are. I don't normally do an amniocentesis stat, but I think seeing how grief-stricken you are, it would be best if you knew as soon as possible. If you'd like to have it done today, I will do it."

We agreed, with some hesitation, to go ahead and have the test done. Dr. Doyle assured us that there was a minimal risk of miscarriage. Gene and I both felt that it was important to know what syndrome the baby may have, not only to prepare for what care may be needed for the baby, but also for us as a family to be as emotionally prepared as we could. The possibility of us being anywhere near emotionally prepared seemed extraordinarily bleak.

I had the amnio that very day. It didn't really hurt as much as I thought it would. The doctor inserted a very long needle into my uterus through my abdomen to extract some of the amniotic fluid. They would later test the fluid to determine exactly if and what chromosome disorder it was. We were told we would have to wait two weeks for the results. We left the office feeling overcome with fear and sadness. On the journey home, Gene and I came to a decision to not tell the children about the baby until we knew exactly what was wrong.

"It's gonna be the longest two weeks of our lives," I said as I stared out the car window. "How are we gonna look at Paul and Grace in the face? They think everything is okay."

"Jane, we can't tell them, you know that. We'll get through it!" Gene sounded angry. "You better pull yourself together before we go in the house, you can't let the kids see that you've been crying," he said, rather authoritatively.

"Why are you being so mean to me, Gene?" I whined.

Marge had been quiet up to that point. "Kids, kids, you are both in pain right now. As hard as it is, you need to be supporting each other right now." Neither one of us responded, and Marge said nothing more.

కోల

When we walked into the house Grace and my dad were sitting at the table playing a game called War with a deck of cards. Mom was sitting on the couch saying her prayers. Dad looked up at me and didn't say a word. I'm sure he could tell by the look on my face that the news wasn't good. Somehow he knew enough not to say anything in front of Grace.

"Hey, Grandma Marge, what are you doing here?" Grace jumped up and gave her a big hug.

"Hi, baby, I came to go to the doctor with your parents."

"Oh, how was it?" Grace asked while staring at me looking puzzled. "Are you okay, Mommy?"

"Yes, I'm fine, I'm just really tired. You know how I get at this time of day."

"That's why I'm going to take off now," Marge said.

" Oh, Grandma, so soon?" Grace whimpered.

"Yes, baby, but I'll be back again this week, I promise."

Marge said her goodbyes to all of us and left. We sat down to what would normally be a delicious meal to me, but I didn't eat it. It consisted of my dad's famous breaded chicken cutlets, roasted red potatoes with garlic, and steamed broccoli. Gracie and my parents seemed to enjoy it (Paul too, with the exception of the chicken), while Gene and I sat there quiet. It was an effort to speak, but I managed to, for Paul and Grace's sake. Soon it was time for the kids to go to bed.

Grace blessed the baby, as she did every night. It took all I had not to burst into tears when she did it. With Paul and Grace upstairs, we now had the opportunity to share all of the news with my parents the horrible possibilities that we, and especially our baby, faced.

"Oh, Jane." Mom whispered with sadness.

Dad sat there with his head down and his arms folded, as he always did when deep in thought or despair.

My mother spoke up again. "What will you do, dear?" I think she was waiting for me to say I wasn't going to have an abortion.

"You know Gene and I would never terminate the pregnancy."

Gene stood up abruptly and stated, "Well, I'll tell you what else I'm not going to do, and that's to stand by and have my baby suffer, and then watch my children at their own brother or sister's funeral."

"Well, that isn't our choice Gene; I thought you felt the same way I did."

"That was before I found out what this baby might have to endure, only to die anyway!" he shouted back. My parents gazed at him with surprise and sympathy. It was so unlike him to lash out like that. It was totally understandable under the circumstances. "I'm out of here," he said, and stormed out of the house. We heard him pull away.

I couldn't cry another tear. I just gazed into my parent's faces. "What do I do?"

"You go upstairs and try your best to get some sleep, dear," my mother said as she took hold of my hand. "You've had a long and difficult day."

I looked back at her. "I will, but I need to talk about this. I know it sounds horrible but in a way I wish I believed in abortion. Gene is right. How can we go through this only to give birth to an innocent little baby that could suffer and then die? Part of me wishes God would just take the baby from me now."

Dad looked up at me. "I don't blame you, Jane; I don't want you and Gene to have to endure this either. It's awful, it's beyond awful."

"You don't know what's wrong yet. For now you can only pray about it," Mom stated gently.

"I'm worried about Gene," I replied.

"You have to give him some time," my dad continued. "Jane, Gene is a man who takes such good care of his family. He wants to be able to take care of this baby, to fix things, so to speak. He can't, he knows that. He's not only feeling the grief you are, but also a great amount of frustration. Just give him time, Jane."

"I know, I know, Dad." I stood up and said my goodnights to both of them. "I have to go make some dreaded phone calls before bed. Thanks for listening, and for your sound advice. Try to get some sleep, too"

I went to my room and made the necessary phone calls, to my siblings, and very close friends. One conversation stuck out in my mind; it was one I had with my brother Tommy.

"Tommy, one of the things that's eating me alive since we got the news that there was something wrong is looking at Paul and Grace, and how this will affect them. I didn't sleep a wink last night thinking about them. Dad didn't sleep last night either."

There was silence. Tommy broke it by saying, "It's worse for Mom and Dad."

Astonished at his remark, I gasped. "What? What do you mean?"

"Don't get me wrong, the situation isn't harder on them, but their worries for you have to be very difficult. Remember Jane, you are their child, and even though Paul and Grace will be affected by all of this, they will grow up and move on. This will be yours and Gene's life now. It's hard for Mom and Dad to watch you go through this. I'm not trying to make you feel bad. I just don't want you to be overcome with worry about the kids. If you're okay, they'll be okay. Do you know what I mean?"

"Yeah, Tommy. Thanks. You made me feel a little better about the children."

"Jane, Mom, and Dad will be okay, too, they'll get through it like they have gotten through everything else. Everyone's main concern is you and Gene. We're all here for you, you know?"

"I do, Tom, thanks so much. Love you"

"You too, kiddo. Goodnight."

I never heard Gene come in to bed that night. I woke up around 2 a.m. with severe pains in my legs. The pains seemed to be getting worse each night. I got out of bed and made my way to our bathroom medicine cabinet to take some Tylenol, as I did every night for the next few weeks to follow. I went back to bed and lay awake for hours, imagining the very worst and thinking about how Gene and I would share it with the children. Although my brother Tommy's words gave me some relief in regards to the kids, it felt so much worse in the stillness and darkness of the night. I was literally shaking through each thought, anxious for the light of day.

Chapter Nineteen

The weeks that followed seemed like an eternity, with the occasional breaks of hope from well-wishers and lots of prayers. We had many visitors in those two weeks; people dropping off food, flowers, and gifts. It touched our hearts knowing how many people cared about us. We always made sure the children were not around when receiving visitors, and if they were, we didn't discuss the baby. One afternoon, Gene's Aunt T came to visit, along with his (our) Aunt Mary and Uncle Gary. I recall all of us sitting in the den with the fireplace crackling, everyone being sympathetic and trying to sound positive at the same time.

It was so awkward for everyone. Then Aunt T said something so incredibly profound to us. "Gene and Jane," she said in a quiet voice, "no matter what happens, no matter what affliction your child may have, he will never offend God." Those words meant so much to me; my child would always be an innocent. Whenever I would well up with fear, I would think of that powerful statement. Somehow it helped me.

❧

The day came for my parents to go back to their home. I hated them leaving, but I knew that they needed to. As feeble as my mother was, she still managed to play the piano in a band. She had already given up a few gigs in order to spend that time with us, and had even missed a few doctors' appointments, which she really shouldn't have done. The car was packed, and Gene was ready to take them to the airport.

"Just think. One more day, honey, and you will have the results. Call us as soon as you hear," Dad said as he embraced me. Crying, I looked over at my mother.

"It will be okay dear, we'll be praying," She said, then hugged me as well.

"I wish you were going to be here when I get the results," I sniffled. "I guess that it's best that it's just the four of us here when we find out."

"I definitely think so, Jane. You need to have that alone time with Paul and Grace, it's better for them."

"I know you're right, mom, I'll miss you both," I said through my veil of tears.

"We'll miss you too, dear."

I know she hated the goodbyes as much as I did, especially in this situation. I helped walk my mom to the car and into the back seat. I buckled her in, kissed her on the cheek, and shut the car door. Gene pulled out of the driveway as we waved goodbye to each other. Boy, did that hurt.

D-day had arrived with our breakfast being as typical as it always was. At least it was for Paul and Grace. They had no idea what was about to unfold that day. Neither did Gene and I, for that matter. We had left Gene's phone number with the genetic counselor, Susan, feeling it was best that when the results came in, Gene would be the best person to contact. He was worried about my initial reaction to the results, especially if I was alone.

I was too shaky to venture out anywhere that day, so I busied myself with household chores, some reading, and a little T.V., but not without calling Gene several times to see if he had heard anything. There were moments that day, like every other day for the last two weeks, that I had wondered what scenario would be worse. With the exception of nothing being wrong at all, of course. Each syndrome presented to us, even Turners and Downs, scared me beyond belief. All I could think of was however this pregnancy turned out; our lives would be changed forever. I felt angry. As selfish as that may sound, it's how I really felt.

I was standing at the kitchen sink finishing up my lunch dishes when I heard Gene's van pull into the driveway, a sound I listened for usually at the end of the day. It was only 2 p.m. He was home early, which could only mean one thing. He had received the news, and it wasn't good or he would have called me. I walked over to the window and watched him as he walked up the slate pathway with his head down. Oh no, I thought. As he opened the door, I looked at him. He was visibly upset, and could barely look at me.

I almost didn't ask, because I already knew it in my heart. "It's Down Syndrome, isn't it?"

"Yes," he said, almost sounding like he was sorry. Oh God, oh God. I began to walk quickly, pacing, wanting to run away from it. Why I did what I did I don't know, but I walked toward the bathroom screaming. I began to bang on the closed door as hard as I could.

"Please, please, God, take my arms, anything, but don't make me tell my children this news, please!"

Gene was behind me at that point, holding me up by my elbows as I began to collapse on the floor. We both sat on the floor, Gene holding me and telling me everything would be alright as I cried once again. I'm ashamed I was such a mess, but I had no control over my feelings at that point. I kept thinking that our lives were over. We would have a child that would always be a child, worse yet, one that would be picked on and ridiculed. It tore my heart out. I had a lot to learn yet.

Eventually I regained my composure. Gene helped me off of the floor. We sat on the couch for a while, talking about what we should do next. Our first thought was how to tell the children. Once they heard the news we wanted them to have the choice to be with us at home, or maybe visit with a friend, someone they could vent to besides Gene and I.

I went ahead and called a couple of their closest friends' parents, informed them of the news and asked them if it would be okay if they visited their homes if that's what Paul and Grace had decided to do. I knew beyond doubt that it wouldn't be a problem. We then decided to contact a school that provided early intervention for children with Down syndrome. Susan had passed along the number to us, so we went ahead and called. We were able to make an appointment for the very next day. Obviously, we made the necessary phone calls to family and friends. It took a tremendous amount of energy to rehash it over and over again.

Paul arrived home from school first, as he always did. I had his grilled cheese waiting for him. "Hey Ma," he said as he took his coat off and hung it on the banister.

"Can you hang that up, please?"

" Yeah, in a minute."

"It's always in a minute, do it now!"

I guess I sounded really aggravated because he hung it

up with no more feedback. He sat down at the island to eat his sandwiches. "I'm going to Chris' house to jam, can you drive me?"

"Not today, and you'll need to hang around here until Grace comes home. Dad and I need to talk to you."

Paul was annoyed. "Oh, c'mon. What now? I told Chris and Brian I could play today." He banged his fist on the island.

"I don't want to hear it," I yelled back, feeling extremely sad and stressed out. "We need to talk to you and Grace, maybe when we're done you can go to Chris'." What Paul didn't know was that I had just spoken to Chris' mom, in regards to him going there as an option.

"Okay, Mom. Whatever." He took the last bite of his sandwich and stormed up the stairs. "Call me when Grace gets home."

"How about, thanks for the sandwiches, Mom?" I said back sarcastically.

"Thanks for the sandwiches." I could tell he felt bad. I was angry about his attitude, but knew he didn't know what was about to be told to him. This time it was easy to forgive his teenage angst. Another half-hour and Grace would be home, and then we could get those dreadful moments over with. I decided to spend the time praying the Rosary, while Gene busied himself by straightening out the basement. It was unorganized because of me. I had a hard time parting with sentimental things; the basement was chock-a-block full of "stuff". Being that Gene was a bit of a neat freak, it naturally drove him nuts. So, occasionally he would go down there and weed things out. It was therapeutic for him, as my prayer was for me. We both did what we needed to do. To each his own, as the saying goes.

Grace finally walked in the door wearing her backpack and her cheerful disposition. "Hey Mom," she said as she came over and kissed me. "Is Dad home? Why is his van in the driveway?" Immediately my heart started to race, and I felt sick to my stomach.

"Yes, Dad is home, he got out of work early. I was just about to go down stairs and get him. Honey, Dad and I need to talk to you and Paul about something. Would you mind getting your brother for me? He's in his room."

"Sure, Mom. Is everything okay?" she asked with sincere concern.

"We just need to talk to the two of you." My voice started to shake, so I just turned away from her and walked towards the basement door as she started to walk up the stairs to get Paul.

Gene was finishing up when I got down there. "They're both home. Are you ready? Do you want me to explain, or do you want to?"

"I guess you can start and we'll just see how it goes."

We walked up the basement stairs to find both of them sitting on the couch. The same couch we had videotaped them on two and a half months before, with Grace jumping up and down and Paul grinning from ear to ear. Ugh, how am I going to say this to them?

My knees became weak, so I sat down next to Grace. Gene stood there, cleared his throat, holding back his tears, and said, "Mom and I have some upsetting news to share with you." Their eyes followed his as he looked over at me.

I sat there rubbing my hands together, as if I was trying to wash all of it away. My anxiety was through the roof. "Well, two weeks ago, Dad and I went to the doctor. They gave me a sonogram, and found something on the back of the baby's head. It's called a cystic hygroma."

Grace looked at me puzzled. Paul looked the same and asked, "WHAAAT? What the heck does that mean?" I grabbed hold of Grace's hand, she was obviously upset.

"Well," Gene said, "it could have meant several things, some of them beyond terrible. We found out today, after waiting two weeks for the test results that your brother or sister has Down syndrome."

Immediately Grace started to sob. Paul just sat there staring into space.

"We're not sure how this is going to turn out. There are some things medically wrong with the baby because of the hygroma and the Down syndrome."

"Like what?" Grace asked through her tears.

"Sometimes there can be problems with the baby's heart or kidneys," I told her. "We'll know more the further along I am in the pregnancy."

Gene went over and put his hand on Paul's back, while Grace continued to cry softly.

"It could be so much worse. A boy in my school has a brother that can't speak or walk. He'll never be out of a wheelchair," Paul stated with a convincing tone. I sat there in awe. Here's our son, just turned 15 years old, looking at the realities of the positive side of our situation. He was grateful that Down syndrome was all he had.

"Wow, Paul," Gene said, "what a way to look at it." Grace looked up at him in disbelief, too.

"Gracie," I asked, "are you okay?"

"Not really, I feel sorry for the baby," she cried.

"I know honey, me too." I hugged her.

She patted my back. "I'm okay Mom," she said as she wiped her big blue swollen eyes.

"Is there anything you kids want to ask us, or talk about?" Gene asked.

Paul turned towards Gene. "When will you know if there is anything wrong with the heart or kidneys?"

"Mom will be having another sonogram, probably at her next doctor's visit. They can keep track of what's going on that way. We'll know more and more as time goes on." Gene paused. "Tomorrow Mom and I are going to visit a school for children with Down syndrome. We thought we should start looking into things for the baby right away."

Both of the children sat there, nodding their heads in approval. We were all silent for a few moments. There was an occasional sniffle here and there.

"Dad and I weren't sure how you would take this news. We, as a family, have a long road ahead of us. So, for right now, we wanted you to be okay and comfortable. We would love you to be here with us right now, to vent or even to go to your own rooms and be by yourselves. We also wanted you to have the opportunity to leave for a few hours if you'd like. I went ahead and called Shannon and Chris' moms to see if it was okay to go spend time with them, if that's what you choose to do. They're waiting for your phone calls."

"I think I'd like to go to Chris'."

"I think I'd like to go to Shannon's, but I don't want you

two to feel bad," Grace added.

"Hey," Gene said, "We have plenty of time to talk about this, we don't feel bad, we just want you kids to be okay."

"Dad's right. Why don't you call your friends, either Dad or I will drop you off."

Paul came over to hug me. "Those kids seem so loyal and loving, Mom, don't worry."

I was dumbfounded and ever so grateful. He would never know what those words meant to me, especially in those difficult moments. He was just 15, and amazing. Grace got up with her bloodshot eyes and gave me a kiss on the cheek. She was like me in regards to hugs, afraid to burst into tears again.

"Okay, kinder, you go get ready!"

They both slowly walked up the stairs. Gene and I stood there gazing at each other, shaking our heads. I got up and walked over to him. We embraced. Tears of relief drizzled down my face. If they were okay, I would be okay. We decided it would be best if Gene took them to their friends. I was emotionally drained and in no shape to drive. Besides, Gene had to stop by the firehouse to do some paperwork, anyway. He also decided that he would pick up some dinner for us on the way home.

I made some more phone calls. I made two calls to my parents, the first one to give them the results of the amnio, the second to tell them of Paul and Grace's response to the news.

"Hello, Mom?"

"Oh, yes Jane, I guess you told the children?"

"Yeah, we did."

"How are they?"

"You would be so proud of them, Mom. They actually made me feel better. Paul in so many words said how we all should be grateful it wasn't worse. How his friend's brother would never be able to get out of a wheelchair. Of course, Grace is in a place I thought she would be. She's feeling sorry for the baby. She did seem better than I thought she would be, though."

"Oh, Jane, you must feel so much better that they know."

"I can't tell you, Mom. I feel like heavy weights have been lifted off my shoulders. You know how scared I am. Those feelings haven't changed much, but the children knowing what's going on has made it so much more bearable for me, especially because of the way they reacted. I know that must sound crazy."

"No, it doesn't, honey, you've been carrying this secret with you for weeks. That had to be torture, especially with the uncertainty of it all. At least now you know that the baby has Down syndrome."

"Some of the uncertainty is still there, honestly the fear is too, but it's eased a bit."

"I'm sure as time passes you'll learn more about all of this. As you do, your fear will lessen. Keep praying, honey."

"Oh, you know I've been, Mom. Of course, Grace has been blessing the baby every day. My friend Patty has blessed the baby too, with holy water from the St. Padre Pios shrine. Our families and our friends have been so good to us. I get a different card in the mail every day. Yesterday my friend Kelly left a prayer book for me on our front steps. My friend Terri baked brownies for us. The list goes on and on. It's as though all of them would do anything to make us feel better."

"You and Gene are very blessed, Jane."

"I know we are. As bad as I feel about our situation, I keep thinking about my friends and family who just had a baby or are pregnant now. I'm sure I told you, Bridgette across the street just had a healthy little girl. My friends Kelly and Dawn and two of Gene's cousins are expecting. Three of them are due within weeks of me. I know they all feel terrible about our baby. It's probably hard for them to be excited about their own baby in front of us. On the other hand, I would be a liar if I said I'm not jealous of them. I'm happy that they are having healthy babies, but I wish I was having one, too. That's terrible, isn't it?"

"No, Jane, it's not terrible, it's a normal way to be feeling. I would feel the same way. You aren't wishing harm on any of them. You just want what they have. Right now you need to take care of yourself, though. All of that other stuff will take care of itself, Jane."

"I know you're right, Mom."

Just then Gene walked in with a bag of fast food in his

hand.

"Oh, Mom? Gene just walked in with dinner, can I call you back?"

"Oh no, dear, you go eat. I'll let Dad know that you told the children. I bet you'll sleep better tonight knowing what's going on, and that the children know too. I know Dad and I will sleep better."

"I hope so. I think I'll actually be able to eat my dinner tonight, too. Well, goodnight Mom, love you. Please give Dad a big hug for me, and assure him that I'm feeling better about everything."

"I will, dear. God bless you, Jane"

"Mm hmm, you too, Mom."

I actually did eat my whole meal that night. It consisted of a grilled chicken sandwich and french fries. I know, not the healthiest of dinners, but it tasted good. It was the most I had eaten at one time in weeks. The children were dropped off by 8 p.m. That night, Grace asked me if I would lay down with her until she fell asleep. How could I refuse? She got herself ready for bed then shouted down to me, "Mom, I'm in bed now."

"Okay, Grace, I'm coming."

I climbed the stairs and walked into her room. She looked so tiny lying there under her floral quilt. She was staring at the ceiling.

"Can I turn the light off, Grace?"

"Sure."

I lay down next to her on the bed. "Are you all right, sweetie?"

"I guess. I keep on thinking about what the baby will be like. I used to wonder who it would look like, now it won't look like any of us. I feel so bad for thinking like that. I know it's not important."

"Don't feel bad about what you're thinking and feeling. It's so good that you can talk about it. The truth is, Grace, I'm thinking about those things, too. There are so many things I'm thinking about, that was just one of the thoughts that ran through my head."

"There are people with Down syndrome in my school; it's so hard to understand them when they talk. I'm afraid people will make fun of our baby." She started to cry.

"Oh, Gracie, those fears are real and understandable. There are many things this child will have to face, and we so will we. We'll get through it as a family. I can promise you this baby will do wonderful in life, in part because he'll have you for a sister and Paul for a brother." She continued weeping. "It's okay to cry, I've done plenty of it." I rubbed her back for a while until she fell asleep. My poor Gracie. I quietly got up and went into Paul's room to say goodnight. He was already fast asleep. Emotionally it was a tough day for everyone, we were all exhausted.

Chapter Twenty

After a 35 minute ride, we made a right off of the main road onto a side street, which was where the special needs school was supposed to be. It didn't look right; it was a residential neighborhood. The woman that gave us directions said it would be at the end of the road. We kept driving, thinking we went the wrong way, but then, there it was. A brick school building set back on a large piece of property. It had a circular driveway in front of it. The sign in front said, "A Place of Hope and Opportunities for Children with Down Syndrome", written big in primary colors. What a strange feeling it was to approach a facility such as that, knowing it was a school our child may one day attend. Things like that happened to other people, like Billy's (from Emmets Farms) parents, not to us. Now maybe I would be packing a snoopy lunch box for a grown man some day. We parked the car and walked to the main doors. There was an intercom attached to the brick wall with a button next to it. Gene pushed the button.

A woman's voice came out of the box. "Can I help you?"

Gene replied, "Yes, we have an appointment for a tour of the school, Gene and Jane Spiotta."

"Sure, Ill buzz you in."

We walked through the heavy glass doors into the foyer, and it smelled like any other school. To the right of us was a wall lined with metal framed chairs with royal blue cushions. In front of us were two large wooden doors that looked like they probably lead to a gymnasium or auditorium. To the left of us was a reception area and office. Glass separated us from the woman behind it. She was sitting at a desk, and she stood up and leaned over to slide the glass door over.

"Good morning," the smiling Hispanic woman said.

"Good morning," we both replied, feeling nervous.

"You said you were here for a tour. I'll let Marilyn know you're here. Do me a favor and sign in." She handed us a clipboard with a sign-in sheet, then gave us adhesive name tags to put on, which had our names on them, written in black magic marker. "I'm sure Marilyn will be with you shortly."

"Ok, thanks," Gene said. We signed in and had a seat; neither of us spoke. Not even five minutes had passed when we saw a tall thin woman walking toward us. She appeared to be in her upper fifties with chin-length salt and pepper hair cut bobbed style. Sophisticated was how she appeared, and the brown tweed suit she was wearing added to her "look".

"Mr. and Mrs. Spiotta?" she asked, grinning as she reached out to shake our hands.

"Yes, Gene and Jane," Gene politely answered.

"Hi, I'm Marilyn. I'm one of the social workers here. Welcome. Now, from what I understand, you just found out you're having a child with Down syndrome. I know that must have been difficult for you to hear. Hopefully after visiting our school and seeing how wonderful these children are, it will ease your fears a bit. Come on, let me show you around."

We started to walk down the main corridor. There was so much to look at. I spotted what resembled a wagon. It was red, with three rows of red and white striped seats in it. "What is that for?" I asked Marilyn.

"Oh, that's just to transport the children to and from the bus. We use it for the real little ones who can't walk yet, to transport them from their classrooms, and sometimes the music room or the cafeteria."

Then I noticed many photographs lining the walls. They were photos of beautiful little children, mostly with Down syndrome. One was of a pretty baby girl on a swing with a big smile on her face, and the little bit of blonde hair she had was blowing in the wind. It was a truly captivating picture.

"This is the parent lounge," Marilyn said as she pointed into the room. No one was in there, but there were a bunch of chairs surrounding a coffee table with a pile of magazines on it.

"Many of the parents who drive their children here will sit in here while their child is having services."

"Services?" I asked.

"Yes, occupational therapy, physical therapy, and speech. All of the children start out with those services. How often and how long they will need them depends on their progress."

"When do they start these therapies?" I inquired.

"We can start your child at six weeks old."

"Six weeks? What does a baby at six weeks old do with speech?" Gene asked confused.

Marilyn went on. "Well, we are not actually teaching them to speak. We do, however, speak to them and use sign language at the same time. Children with Down syndrome have low muscle tone, some more severe than others. Either way, our tongues are muscles. Their tongues aren't as strong as ours. We teach you ways to help strengthen their mouths so they are able to speak better, and also eat easier. The earlier you begin with all of these therapies the better off your child will be."

I looked at Gene. "How are we gonna to pay for all of this?"

"Pay?" Marilyn asked. "You don't pay anything. These children are entitled to all of this through the state." Oh, I guess I should have known that.

We continued to walk down the hall. "This is the music room. You can peek in if you want."

I looked through the small panel of glass that was on the door. There was a woman sitting at the piano. Freckles covered her square face, and tight curly hair sat on top of her head. She was grinning big as she sang "The Wheels on the Bus", and accompanied herself on the piano as she sang. Then I noticed all of the babies, all sitting on adults' laps, presumably their mothers. Some were clearly not affected by the music, while some were bopping in time to it. As I looked at each child, I couldn't help but think that Grace was right; these children didn't look like their mothers. I couldn't even tell if they were or not. All of these children looked like each other. As shallow and awful as it sounds, that's how I felt at the moment, I'm not proud of it. I walked away briskly with Gene and Marilyn following behind; they obviously knew I was upset.

Gene caught up to me and put his arm around me. "What's the matter, are you okay?"

"No I am not. I honestly don't know if I can do this. Gene, this is just too much." I began weeping again for the zillionth time. I was so sick of crying, I can only imagine how it made Gene feel to watch it day after day. He never made me feel bad about it.

Marilyn was walking on the other side of me. "I know you're probably still in a little bit of shock over this, after all you only found out yesterday. You need to give yourself time, and you have plenty of it. Try to be patient with yourself. Maybe you can start to do some research from home, just a little at a time."

"I agree," Gene said. "Thanks, Marilyn." I didn't say a word. "Let me take you home, Jane, we'll come back at a later time."

I got my composure. "No, I'm okay. Let's keep going."

"You're sure?" Gene asked.

"I'm sure."

Marilyn continued to give us the tour. We were able to meet many of the staff, who were all eager to answer any questions, and who were clearly wonderful with the children. As we walked past the parent lounge again, I noticed three women sitting in there. They were all laughing about something. It struck me in a positive way that they were laughing. It gave me hope that I would someday enjoy simple conversation again. Up until that point I couldn't picture ever feeling like myself again. Before we left the school, Marilyn was nice enough to give us some brochures of the school, and even a few websites we could visit to get more information and gain knowledge for this new world we were embarking on.

"Here is something else I think may help you a little. It's a beautiful poem, written by Emily Perl Kingsley. It's called, "A Trip to Holland". Hold on to it and read it when you think you're ready; it sends a powerful message."

"Thank you, Marilyn. I'm sorry about my little break down before, it seems to be becoming a habit lately."

"No worries. As I said, you're still in shock. In time it will get better, especially when you have your baby in your arms. Remember, Gene and Jane, you aren't having a Down syndrome child, you're having a child that happens to have Down syndrome. It will all be okay, you'll see."

෨ৣৎ

Marilyn was right. After the shock of it all, and after learning more about Down syndrome, I started to feel better.

I actually began to get back to doing normal things. Having lunch with friends, shopping, visiting with family and friends on weekends, and yes, even laughing! Of course, the constant support from our loved ones and strangers alike blew my mind, but mostly touched my heart. I don't think that more than two days would go by without a card or letter coming in the mail for us. My sister Tess even had a prayer hotline going for us.

I think what affected me most were the phone calls and letters we received from our young nieces and nephews. My 13-year-old goddaughter Jamie wrote to me and told me how proud she was of me for having her cousin, and how loved the baby would be. Another niece of mine, Liz, called me and told me how she'd been taking a walk with her sister Rebecca and said to her, "I know everyone is upset about Aunt Jane and Uncle Gene's baby, but truthfully I'm kind of excited about having a child like that in our family."

My brother Dave's daughter Jenny said to him, "Aunt Jane and Uncle Gene's baby will be the perfect ending to our family," knowing he would undoubtedly be the last grandchild.

Out of the mouths of babes. How could I not, even through my fear, be grateful?

Chapter Twenty One

It was time for my next visit to our regular OB/GYN. I was to see a Dr. Williams. Gene and I waited patiently in the waiting room. Finally, Dr. Williams entered the room.

"Hello there," he said, "I'm Dr. Williams." We both looked up at him. He was well over six feet, average weight, and he had a strong nose and silver hair. "So, I read your records. Your baby has a few problems. The first being Downs, which of course can coincide with many medical issues. Secondly, the baby has a cystic hygroma"

"We know all of that, doctor. Did you read the sonogram report?" Gene asked.

"Yes, I did. You know there's a good chance you won't carry this pregnancy to full term. With those two significant problems, the baby is in trouble."

I looked at him puzzled. "Well, what are the statistics?"

"There aren't any. Are you both sure you want to have this baby?"

"Yes, we are sure." Gene answered adamantly.

"Okay, then." He proceeded to measure my stomach, jotted some stuff down on my chart, and went to leave the room. "I'll see you in four weeks, be sure to take your vitamins."

"Hey, Doc," Gene said before he could leave.. "I'm afraid Jane might become depressed, can she take medication if she needs to?"

I looked at Gene, feeling appalled. "What? I don't need medication."

"She can take anything she wants. Call me if you need a script. You're a brave couple." He left and shut the door behind him.

At that point I didn't know who I felt like smacking, the doctor or Gene. The doctor for being so abrupt, though I should have been grateful he didn't try to talk me into an abortion, or Gene for speaking for me in regards to medication. It was as if I wasn't even there.

"Why would you ask him that, Gene? I'm down because

of the circumstances, I don't need medication to numb me from what our reality is, but maybe you do. I'll get through this without it, thank you very much!"

"Well, you don't seem to be getting through it okay, you're always crying. Forgive me for being concerned, I was only trying to help!" he shouted back at me.

We walked out of the office not speaking a word to each other. It wasn't the first or the last time we would lash out at one another throughout that difficult time, and each time we vowed to try to have more patience. Oh well, our intentions were good.

It seemed we lived in the doctor's office for the first few months of knowing about the baby's condition. There I was, at Dr. Doyle's again, this time for another level 2 sonogram. At that point I was about five months along. They would be able to see much more in the way of the baby's health. We decided as a family before even going to see Dr. Doyle that we would like to know the gender of the baby. Our sentiment was that we would like to give our child a definite identity and name in case something did happen to him or her. All along I felt it was a boy, while Gene and the children thought it was a girl. We had already picked names. It would be Thomas William for a boy, after my brother and dad, and Theresa Christine for a girl, after two of my sisters.

Gene and I arrived at the office to meet Susan, our genetic counselor. She wanted to be there for the sonogram I would be having. She was sitting in the waiting room when we walked in. "Hey, guys." she stood up and gave us both a hug. It's amazing how close you can get with the professionals that walk through a crisis with you. You sometimes form a special bond. We actually felt like Susan was our friend.

"Hi Susan, we're glad you're here," Gene said.

"Thanks for letting me share in it. You know your letting me share in this journey with you may someday be beneficial to another couple who could be in same situation as you."

I was happy to hear those words. "Hey, Gene and I were wondering if you could tell us the gender of the baby."

"You want to know?" She held the closed folder she had in her hand over her chest. She whispered, "It's a boy."

"It's Thomas William," I said softly. I looked over at Gene. He had tears rolling down his cheeks.

"It's a boy," he said with his lips quivering. I didn't know if they were tears of joy, or tears of sadness. Probably both. There was no need to ask, he would have reacted the same way if it was a girl. I took hold of his hand when the office door opened.

"Mrs. Spiotta?" a young girl in pink scrubs inquired. All three of us stood up and followed her into a very large room. Dr. Doyle was already in there, along with Kathryn the sono tech.

"Hello there, folks," he exclaimed with a smile. "Boy, you look a lot better than last time you were here. That was a tough day. How are you feeling now?"

"Good, Doctor. We just found out that we're having a little boy. Now we just want to hear that he is medically healthy."

"Well, let's take a look."

As Kathryn began to slide the wand across my belly, the doctor once again started to explain things to us. He began with Thomas' little feet. "I don't know if you can see that there is a little separation between his first and second toe, which is a typical marking of Downs." Kathryn looked as though she was taking measurements of everything. "There are his legs. They look average size so far. There are his hands." She showed us his fingers "Three bones in each pinky. Sometimes these children only have two." Then she went to the spine and back. Dr. Doyle commented, "See, there is the hygroma, it appears that it has decreased in size.

"That's great," I said. They checked his heart and his kidneys.

"Everything is okay, and pretty much the same, although as I said, the hygroma looks smaller. His heart and kidneys look okay, still a little soon to say he is 100% in the clear, but I'm optimistic."

"Doctor?" Gene asked. We know that even though things were looking up, there is still a chance we may lose him. We believe it was all happening for a reason. "If we do lose him, will we be able to donate his organs?"

I looked at Gene in shock, not knowing that those thoughts ever even entered his mind.

"Although that is admirable and touching that you would entertain those thoughts right now, because of his syndrome they would reject his organs. I'm so sorry."

Gene put his head down. "It's okay, I understand."

At that moment I wanted to jump off the table and wrap my arms around him. The journey we had been on for only four months seemed like an eternity. Gene wanted and needed a reason, a purpose for the pain. I totally understood. What a heart he had. He wanted to help someone else. What a feeling to know your baby's organs wouldn't be good enough. Talk about feeling defeated. My heart broke for Gene and for our son.

Susan broke the silence. "Well, that was good news about the hygroma."

"Yes, it was," I agreed. Now we can go home and tell Paul and Grace the positive news, along with telling them they're going to have a little brother."

Dr. Doyle said his goodbyes. "We'll check on the baby again in two months. You know if anything changes, or if you have any questions, to call me."

"Yes, Doctor, thank you, and thank you, Kathryn," I said.

"No problem, good luck to you."

"Thanks." Gene waved.

ॐ०ॐ

We reached home about ten minutes before Grace did. Paul was downstairs playing his drums, he didn't even hear us come in; he couldn't have over the sound of them. I prepared a snack for Paul and one for Grace as well. Paul must have smelled it, because before I was done preparing them, the drumming stopped and he was standing in the kitchen behind me. Grace walked in at that moment.

"Hey, Mom," Paul said.

"Hi, Mommy. Dad's here?" Grace asked.

"Yes, he came to the doctor with me today."

"Oh, yeah, how did that go?"

Gene must have heard Paul's question. He was walking down the stairs. "Good," he shared gladly.

"Yeah?" Gracie pleaded with her eyes.

I looked at her with assurance. "Yes, the doctor said the hygroma got smaller. Things are looking better. Guess what we're having?"

"A girl?" they both asked.

"Nope, it's Thomas William." I giggled. We all did.

"No way," Paul spoke as he chewed his sandwich.

Grace put her arms around my thickening waste. "That's great Mommy and Daddy. A boy, wow."

No one could ever know what those moments felt like for me. Still having feelings of apprehension and fear, our children's enthusiasm overpowered any negative thoughts I was feeling. I believe all of us were feeling sheer joy at that moment.

෯෧

I spent most of my free time reading. I read all sorts of books. Books on parenting — on parenting a child with Down syndrome. I read a Nicholas Sparks novel, even self-help books, anything to keep my mind busy when my body wasn't. I do recall one particular fiction novel I read. It took place in the hills of Mississippi in or around 1940. The story was of a woman who gave birth to her fourth child, who happened to have Down syndrome. Back then they didn't call them children with Down syndrome, they called them Mongolian idiots. It sounded, and still does, so barbaric to me, especially because it's true that they called them that. This woman and her family had everything going against them. In those days you didn't attempt to keep your child with a disability, you institutionalized them. If you did decide to keep them, you didn't take them anywhere. There were brave souls that fought for their children and against society's ignorance. Well, this woman was one of those brave souls. She and her family raised this little girl on their own with no help or intervention. They taught her everything; how to eat, walk, get dressed. They tried to teach her to speak. I think the only word she ever spoke was "Mama".

I was touched by the story, not only because of the strides the child made, but mainly by the determination and strength of her mother. It was fiction, but the story held true in many homes, in many parts of the world, since the beginning of time. All I could think of as I read was how blessed I was to have the husband, family and friends that I did, along with all the intervention that was available to our Thomas and to us. I was so grateful I read it.

Chapter Twenty Two

As life began to slowly go back to a relative sense of normalcy, we thought it was time to plan a trip, and decided to visit Tess and Bob. We packed up Gene's Dodge Ram and headed down to the town in Northern Virginia that they resided in. It was a rather pleasant ride. Paul decided to stay back home with his friend Lawrence and his family, which avoided any sibling rivalry on the way down. We decided to take my cousin's daughter Janey with us. She was Grace's age, and more like a sister to Grace than a cousin. Janey was just seven years old when her mother passed away. She and her brother Randy moved in with her grandmother, my beautiful Aunt Jane, and her husband Howard.

My aunt amazed me. She was doing such a great job raising the children, that's why we used to steal Janey once in a while. She was such a delightfully happy little spirit. At one point during the trip, Gene blasted the music on the radio. We were all dancing in our seats, including Gene. As a matter of fact, his moves were the most exaggerated. Occasionally you would hear giggling from the back seat coming from the girls, undoubtedly laughing at Gene. We were all acting silly but having so much fun.

After a six-hour drive, we finally pulled into the driveway of Tess and Bob's home. Kathleen was sitting on the steps in front of their split-level house. She jumped off the steps and ran to the truck, wearing an enormous grin. She was long-legged and thin like Grace and Janie, and was the same age as well. She had shoulder-length dark brown hair, held back with a headband. She had pretty blue eyes.

"Hi, Aunt Jane." she hugged me. Then she walked right over to the girls to hug them also.

"Hey, what about your Uncle Geno?" Gene asked with his arms outstretched.

"Ooh, I'm sorry, Uncle Gene." She giggled and embraced him with a hint of shyness.

"Hey girls, what do you say you help me bring our luggage in now, so we don't have to do it later?"

"Oh, c'mon," Grace whined.

"Gracie, let's just do it now," Janie agreed.

With a bit of resistance they flocked to the back of the truck to collect everything, all of them grabbing all they could to avoid having to come back out again. I gathered all of the trash from inside of the car except the pillows and blankets. Arms full, we walked down the slate walkway and up the steps where we found Tess holding the storm door open. She wore a smile the same as Kathleen. They looked so much alike, only Tess's eyes were green.

"Hey, how was your trip?" She looked at all of our baggage. "You can just put it all in the hallway for now."

"Okay," Gene said. We followed. After placing our things on the floor, we exchanged embraces.

"Look at you, Jane, you look great. You're barely showing."

"That's because of the stress, I guess. I'm certainly eating enough."

"Good, I hope you're hungry now. I fixed some appetizers, and dinner will be ready in another hour or so. Why don't you settle into Kathleen's room? In the meantime, I'll put the appetizers out. I'll meet you in the living room!"

Tess looked at Grace, Janey, and Kathleen. "You girls can have the pull-outs in the living room, is that okay?"

"Great," Grace said, smiling along with the girls.

Gene started to pick up the suitcases. "Where's Bob?"

"Oh, he and the boys are working on a Boy Scout project, they should be home soon."

"Great! Is he off the whole weekend?"

"Yeah, that's why he's working on the project today, so that he could enjoy the weekend with you. Along with being a Lieutenant. Colonel in the United Sates Army, Bob was a devoted husband, father of three, and also a Scoutmaster for my nephews' Ryan and Sean's troop. He was a fabulous brother-in-law, and Godfather to our Paul.

"Hey, speak of the devil," Gene said as he looked at the front door.

"Are you talking about me again?" Bob laughed. Ryan and Sean followed Bob into the house. Before we knew it we all gathered in the living room eating scrumptious appetizers, then around their table for a delicious meal, all made by Tess. Tess never prepared anything that wasn't delicious. It wasn't only the way she cooked, but it was also her presentation with whatever she was serving. She gave her all in everything she did, including every relationship in her life. She was so much like my mother.

"How do you guys feel about going on a hike tomorrow? Do you think you're up to that, Jane?" Bob asked with his arms folded. Everyone turned to look at me.

"How do I say no?" I laughed. "Seriously though, when you say hike, do you mean climbing a big steep mountain, or do you mean taking a walk?"

Bob chuckled. "It's called Great Falls, and while the trails can be a little rocky, I think you can handle it. There'll be a lot of walking as well. It's a beautiful place, and the falls are something to see."

"It's really nice, Jane, I'll think you'll be fine," Tess added.

"Please, Mom?"

"Hey, why do you think I have to be talked into this?" I asked, half-joking. "Sounds good to me, I could use the exercise."

"Okay, then" Bob said. "We'll plan on leaving around 9:00 a.m. Is that okay with all of you?

"Awesome," Gene stated, quite satisfied, as he tipped his chair back, which always made me nuts for fear he would fall. We finished the meal with a Swedish apple pie that I had made the day before. Tess made a crumb cake, both recipes passed down from Mom, and always a hit. We cleaned the kitchen and went back in the living room to watch a movie. If I stayed awake to watch it I might remember what movie they chose. Unfortunately, I had to excuse myself after ten minutes. I couldn't keep my eyes open.

I opened my eyes to a very bright sunny morning. Looking out the window, I knew the air would be crisp. I could almost smell the fresh air. I watched the naked branches on the trees sway in the breeze. A hike, I thought, I don't have anything warm enough, or suitable to wear for a hike. I looked over at Gene, who was sound asleep

I nudged him. "Hey, Geno, We need to get up. It's already 8:00, we need to be ready to leave by 9:00." Poor Gene, having to wake up to me nagging him. He was trying to get his bearings, and I could see he wasn't really too sure of where he was at first. Honestly, I could be so inconsiderate sometimes. He was so patient.

"Okay, I'm getting up," he said, rubbing his eyes.

"Well, I'm gonna get up right now to see if they need any help getting things ready."

"I'm right behind you," he said. I walked in the kitchen. There were some scrambled eggs covered on the counter, with sliced fresh bagels next to them. The smell of coffee filled the air. A full pot was waiting for us. I walked downstairs to the front door. Tess and Bob were already packing the car with a cooler and hiking equipment. I tapped on the glass door. Tess looked up at me, waved, and began to walk towards me.

I opened up the door. "I am so sorry we overslept."

"Don't be silly, you didn't oversleep, we won't be leaving for an hour or so. Everyone is sleeping. Besides, you know Bob, he loves this stuff. He's got all his equipment in the van already."

"Oh, that's great, it'll be fun. Hey, I'm afraid I don't have warm enough clothes to wear. I do have sneakers, but I need something to cover my ears, you know how sensitive they are to the cold, and it looks pretty windy out which makes it worse."

"No worries. I have a nice heavy sweater for you, and a down vest to wear over it. I can give you one of Kathleen's bandanas for your ears. Will that work for you?"

"Sounds perfect."

"Good. Now, why don't you and Gene go fix yourselves something to eat? There are some bagels and eggs. You might have to heat the eggs up. I put a fresh pot of coffee on for you, too. In the meantime, I'll get the kids up and moving so we can get out of here close to 9:00."

That we were—out of the house and on the road by 9:12, to be exact. I checked the clock in the van as we were pulling out of the driveway, feeling rather impressed by our almost perfect timing. "How far is this place from here?" Gene inquired.

"Not far, I'd say about 40 minutes or so. It's a nice ride, but would be nicer in another month or so, when everything starts blooming."

Bob and Gene continued talking, with Ryan sitting in between them. Tess and I chatted in the middle row, with Sean between us. Poor Sean, having to listen to us babbling. He was so adorable, and so quiet. I'm sure it was torture for him to be placed there. There wasn't a word from him. He just looked at the back of Ryan's head, as if to put himself somewhere else. I'm sure the three little girls in the back seat added to Sean's excitement. I knew he wanted to be in the front seat with the guys, but there were no complaints from him. He was so good-natured about everything.

About half way there, Tess tapped Bob's shoulder, then handed him a CD. "Can you put number four on?" Bob slipped the CD into the player.

Tess looked at me and Gracie, and spoke loud enough for Gene to hear. "This song is from me to your Thomas." The music started playing, everyone was silent. The melody was familiar. Phil Collins' voice started to come from the speakers. "You'll be in my heart" was the song, from the soundtrack "Tarzan". I had never listened to the words before. How incredibly fitting they were. We all cried like babies as it played. I was so touched by it. It was a moment I will never forget. I don't think any of us will. My heart was full, and ever so grateful.

Bob was right. Towards the end of our ride, the area was more rural, and pretty to look at. We pulled into a dirt-filled parking lot. A sign stood there that read, "Welcome to Great Falls. Park closes at dusk. Alcoholic beverages prohibited". There was also a map on the sign to inform you where the different trails were. Looking like typical tourists, we all stood in front of the sign and asked a passerby to take our picture. Then we were on our way. Carrying a large backpack that looked like it held everything but the kitchen sink, Bob led the way for all of us. Gene followed Bob with Sean and

Ryan walking beside him. Grace, Janey, and Kathleen walked quickly to keep up with the guys, while Tess and I observed the whole scene.

"The girls look so cute, don't they?" Tess commented. All three of them were wearing bandanas on their heads, like something out of the seventies. All you saw from behind were three skinny little bodies speed walking, all the while gabbing and giggling.

"What a sight. That's probably what we looked like from behind, only we aren't so skinny!" We chuckled. Our tribe followed a dirt path, which eventually led to large boulders and rocks.

"We'll be climbing these size boulders here and there throughout the hike. You think you'll be all right, Jane?" Bob asked as he looked back at me.

"Well, it's worth a shot. You guys'll have to help me climb them, though."

Gene smiled. "Sure, babe."

Bob and Gene climbed up first. It didn't look too difficult. They held out their hands for the children, and then for us. With some effort, I made it. Well, the scene from atop of that boulder was breathtaking. It overlooked the Potomic River, whose color was colonial blue. It was calm in spite of the strong breeze that day, although it displayed periodic white caps. There were two islands in the middle that had several trees on them. The blue and white clouded sky complimented the whole scene. It truly looked like a painting. We were blessed with similar scenery throughout the hike. Halfway through, we decided to rest on a huge rock. Bob took out his little stove and a huge container of Jambalaya. He heated it up and handed each of us a coffee cup full. It hit the spot, so did the cold water we washed it down with. We finished up and were on our way again.

A few things transpired on the rest of our walk. After swishing through some muddy, rocky terrain, Gene pointed to a tree and shouted, "Look, a snake!"

I didn't look, and I smacked him. "Cut it out, Gene, stop teasing me." Of course, everyone but the girls and I laughed.

"Oh my gosh, there is one!" Grace shrieked. I looked over at the tree and saw a big black snake hanging from one of the branches. Needless to say, I wanted to blink my eyes and be back in the van. Unfortunately, I couldn't enjoy the scenery any more. My eyes were above me, to the side of me and on the ground making sure there weren't any snakes. It was when I was looking down I noticed a branch on the ground that was still attached to a tree. It was in the shape of a perfect heart. I wanted to cut it off from the tree and take it with me, but I didn't. I left it there for other people to admire. Hopefully others did as much as me. As I looked at it, I thought of the song "You'll Be in My Heart" — so significant.

By the time we got back into the van I was exhausted. I wasn't the only one. Within ten minutes all of the girls were sound asleep. They slept the entire way home. When we finally arrived, I decided I should probably take a snooze myself. Our plans for that night were to go out to dinner with just the adults, and I wanted to be good company. I decided while trying to fall asleep that late afternoon, that our dinner with Tess and Bob would be the perfect time to ask Tess to be the baby's Godmother.

Tess and Bob chose a steakhouse for us to go to for dinner. It was a neat looking place; Like an old saloon, with rustic barn-wood floors and walls. It was the perfect atmosphere to have an ice-cold beer in a frozen mug. While the guys and Tess could have it, I opted for the next best thing, a root beer in a frozen mug.

"Cheers," Bob said as he raised his mug of beer.

"Cheers," we responded.

"Thanks for a great weekend, what an awesome time we've had." Gene clicked everyone's glass again.

Tess smiled. "Awww, we did, too."

"Tess, Gene and I were wondering if you would do us the honor of being Thomas' Godmother."

"Do you the honor?" She cried tears of joy.

૎૏ૌ

Our ride home that Sunday was quick. It always seemed to be quicker coming home. I was sad to leave Tess and Bob's, but happy about the weekend we shared, so I was content. I left there with the memory of Tess' song of dedication to the baby, the heart-shaped branch we found, and even the snake! Tess accepting our request to be Thomas' Godmother made us so happy. I was full, and ready to go home.

Chapter Twenty Three

Spring came and went quickly. It was the middle of May and time for our last level 2 sonogram. We were once again back in Dr. Doyle's office. This time however, he wasn't there. An associate of his was who we would see. Although I was disappointed, in the end I was glad I had met him. We sat in the familiar room, with me on the examining table. Gene sat on a chair waiting for Kathryn and the doctor.

"Mr. and Mrs. Spiotta? I'm Dr. Colvin." He was a handsome distinguished-looking man with a full head of silver hair, a mustache, and a very kind face. "I'll be standing by to see if there are any significant changes in your baby."

I lay down on the table, and Kathryn began the sonogram. "As you know, the hygroma has slowly gotten smaller. It appears to me that it's decreased in size significantly since your last sonogram."

Gene and I looked at each other with relief.

"There is a chance it could be gone by the time your son is born," Kathryn said, sliding the wand across my stomach.

Dr. Colvin continued, "There are no 100 percent guarantees, but so far everything looks good to me."

"What about his kidneys and his heart?" I asked.

"They appear normal to me. I feel optimistic."

"Oh, that's great, Doctor," Gene stated as he squeezed my hand. Kathryn finished the sonogram.

"Why don't you wash up, then we can have a little chat. I'll be back in a few minutes."

We waited, and in less than five minutes he was back in the room and sitting across from us. "Do you have any questions?"

"So you think our son will be okay?" Gene asked.

"Well," he said, "I think when he's born he'll look like a typical infant. Structurally, his body looks normal. I, myself, know people with Down syndrome. They inherit many of the same traits that your family may have. For instance, if your family is musically inclined there's a good chance he will be as well, or if you're sports oriented, he could be, too. He'll have some of your personality traits; for example, maybe shyness, or a sense of humor, et cetera. Remember, he carries your families' genes."

"Our son plays guitar, do you think he will be able to?"

"I think anything is possible. Can I share something else with you? My thoughts?"

"Of course," I said eagerly.

"Your child might be physically and mentally affected by Down syndrome, but his spirit will never be affected. They are angels."

Gene and I were overwhelmed with emotion by his wise and profound words. I wondered then, and still do, if that man had any idea what that statement meant to Gene and me. They were without a doubt the most impactful words I had heard regarding Thomas and children like him. I am eternally grateful to Dr. Colvin for sharing them with us.

We spent the next month preparing a nursery for Thomas. We gave him the small room across from our newly renovated bedroom, which we did in pale green and lavender; it was a pretty combination. Thomas' room was painted a very light blue. I attempted to paint clouds on the walls, which didn't come out very well, but it would have to do. His carpet was navy blue. We accented it with a white dressing table, dresser, and crib. The dressing table was filled with diapers, bibs, baby wipes, and all the necessary trinkets desired for a newborn. Adorable clothes filled the dresser, compliments of all our family and friends. On top of the dresser sat two music boxes and some pretty frames, and a mother and child statue, all given to me by my mother and sisters. My Aunt Betty knitted a beautiful lemon chiffon colored blanket that lay in the crib. I loved it, especially because my aunt's precious hands made it. Thanks to all of my loved ones, and Gene throwing me a fabulous shower, we were all set.

It was a Thursday night, the next day I would be going for what I thought would be the last visit to Dr. Williams before Thomas would be born. I was ironing the children's clothing when the phone rang.

"Hey Jane, it's Chrissie."

"Hi, Chrissie," I answered enthusiastically.

"I hope you're doing okay."

"I am, as a matter of fact. I have a doctor's appointment tomorrow. Seeing as how I'm due in three weeks, I'm guessing it'll be my last visit, or at least next to last. We have been to so many doctors. I'll be glad when it's over."

"I can't imagine, Jane. Please let me know how it goes tomorrow. Listen, I called because I wanted to tell you about a vision I had about the baby. I know it sounds weird, but it just came to me."

"Tell me, tell me," I pleaded.

"I just saw your house. I walked inside, family and friends filled it. Some followed me into your home. I, along with everyone else, were obviously filled with excitement asking, 'Where is Thomas, where is he?' He was the only one we all wanted to see, and we were all searching for him. We found him playing quietly. He was a few years old, so beautiful, and so happy. We were all thrilled to see him. That was it; that was the image. I felt so peaceful after visualizing that, it made me feel like everything is going to be okay. Maybe it sounds silly."

"Are you kidding? I love that story, Chris. It's beautiful. I think you're right, I think it's yet another sign that everything will be alright. Thanks for sharing it with me."

"Sure, Jane, I'm glad it helped."

"Hey, Gene and I have been trying to reach you and Billy the last couple of days. We wanted to ask Billy to be Thomas' godfather."

"Oh, Jane, that's great." I'll put him on the phone. Can you call me tomorrow after your doctor appointment?"

"Of course, I'll be calling you, and everyone else!"

"Great, I'll put Billy on."

"Thanks, Chris. Love ya. Give the girls a kiss for me."

"Will do. Same here."

A deep southern voice came from the receiver. "Hello.".

"Hey Bill, it's Jane."

"Oh, hey Jane, how are you feeling?"

"I'm feeling much better, especially because it's almost time. It's been a long road, ya know?"

"I can't imagine. We're so glad to hear that the baby is doing okay so far. You know we've been praying for him and for all of you."

"I know, Billy. We've been blessed with the abundance of prayers said for us, and also all the well-wishes."

"I'm sure you are. How are Gene and the kids?"

"All well, thanks. They're as anxious as I am for the baby to be here. Speaking of the baby, that's why I wanted to talk to you. Gene and I would like to know if you would do us the honor of being Thomas' godfather."

"Wow, that would be great! It would be an honor to me. Thank you so much for asking me."

"Wonderful, I'm so glad."

"Me too, Jane"

"I'll be calling you tomorrow to fill you in on my visit with the doctor."

"Great, we'll talk to you then. Give my love to everyone."

"Thanks, Bill. Goodnight."

"Goodnight."

ॐ॰ॐ

Dr. Williams' cold stethoscope was a shock to my belly. He was listening for the baby's heartbeat. It took a while for him to find it. I was relieved when I finally heard the swishing beat, although the look of hesitation on the doctor's face frightened me. "What's wrong?" I asked with a sick feeling in my stomach. He took the stethoscope out of his ears. "Nothing is wrong, but I'd like to do a stress test, and maybe a sonogram."

"Why?" I started to panic.

"Well, the baby has a slower heartbeat than it should. I just want to make sure everything is all right."

"When will you do the tests?"

"I'd like to do them now, since you're already here. Do you have the time?"

"Absolutely, I want to know what is going on."

"It may be nothing. We'll check it out now."

Within one hour both tests were complete, and I was sitting across from Dr. Williams at his desk.

"It appears that your placenta is not nourishing the baby as much as it should. Although the baby is in no immediate danger, I think it's a good idea if we induce your labor at the latest next week. His lungs will be developed by then, they look good now."

"When next week?"

The doctor looked at his calendar. "Would you like a 4th of July baby? I'm on the schedule that day."

"Okay. Are you sure the baby is all right?"

"Yes, I just think he'll get more nourishment from the outside at this point. I'd still like to wait out the week to be sure about his lungs."

"Alright then, the 4th of July it is."

Of course, everyone, especially the children, were excited for him to be born on Independence Day. I was happy as well, but concerned about Thomas; about the nourishment he wasn't getting, and of course, his little lungs. I had to keep trusting.

Chapter Twenty Four

It was the evening of July 3rd. Plans were made for Gene to take me to the hospital. My sister Tess and Gene's sister Mary would be in the delivery room with us, while my sister Kathy, Marge, Grace and Kathleen would come to the hospital when I was in more of an active labor. Paul decided to wait at home until the baby was born. I understood.

I took a shower and gave myself a pedicure. How I reached my toes over my belly, I'll never know, but where there's a will there's a way, and so I managed. Phone calls had been coming in all evening from family and friends, wishing me and Gene their best. One phone call was from Grace's daughter Bethany, who was now a grown woman and a school teacher. Grace would have been so proud of her, of all her children.

"Hi Aunt Jane, it's Bethany."

"Hi, sweetie. How are you?"

"How am I? How are you? Are you ready for the big day?"

"Actually, I'm polishing my toenails. I need to make sure my feet look pretty in those stirrups." I laughed.

"Oh, Aunt Jane, you're ridiculous, too funny! Are you nervous?"

My tone changed. "Yes, honey, I am, but I'll be okay. No worries."

"I do believe everything will be fine. You know Mom is going to be with you, just like she was the first time, just from a different place," Bethany said softly.

"I know, Bethany. I'll be talking to her the whole time." I began to get a little weepy.

"Please know I'll be praying for you, and we'll all be waiting to hear. I love you, Aunt Jane."

"I love you too, Bethany, and thanks for calling."

I had wished all of my family could be with me in the days to come. It especially killed my parents and sister Chrissie not to be there. Mom and Dad asked what I would prefer, to have them come when the baby was born, or after. It was no fault of theirs. I knew if they were at my house when

I just arrived home I would be worried about them. Things were different now. They were older, my mom especially. She would probably need my help as much as I needed hers. Being that Kathy lived next door, and Tess planned on staying for a week, I would have their help as well as Gene's. So for that reason, my parents and Chrissie decided to come later on in the month. My goddaughter Jamie even came from Alabama to help me out for a few weeks. I was surrounded by blessing after blessing.

All of us hurried to get ready when morning arrived. I had to be at the hospital by 6:30 a.m. I think we left the house by 5:30, anticipating a 45-minute drive. We were at St. Mary's Hospital 35 minutes later, the place that our new world would begin.

I was called into the labor room. Gene was allowed to come in with me, while Tess and Mary were asked to wait outside for the time being. "Good morning, honey. How are you doing this morning?" the polite nurse asked.

"I'm okay, a little nervous though." Little did she know how relieved I was that she was so pleasant, which definitely helped in my situation.

"It's no wonder, but I'll take good care of you. Now, I'm going to hook you up to an I.V. for two reasons. Number one, to keep you hydrated, and secondly, to give you the Pitocin drip, which will start your contractions. I'll set all of that up while you change into your gown."

"Okay." I looked at Gene, and gave me a comforting wink.

Before I knew it, the I.V. was in my hand. It was a little painful, but not nearly as bad as the pain I would endure for the next few hours. It wasn't anything I hadn't felt before.

"Jane, I have to ask you," the nurse inquired, "do you want me to order any pain medication for you?"

"No, no thank you though, I had my other children with no medication, I'd like to do the same now."

"Have you ever considered an epidural?"

"No, never. I don't want to take the chance of hurting the baby with meds."

"An epidural will only affect you. It doesn't touch the baby. It's like going to the dentist and not taking Novocain, just to brave it out. I'm not trying to tell you what to do, but if you were my daughter I would recommend it. You don't have to say yes to it now. You can make that choice later as your labor progresses. If you think you might want it, you should sign for it now."

I looked at Gene. "What do you think?"

"Under the circumstances, I would say go for it, but you don't have to have it if you don't want to."

I looked back at the nurse. "You promise it won't affect the baby?"

"It will only give you a tremendous amount of relief."

"Okay then, I'll sign for it.

"Good. As I said, it's only to make it available to you, if you decide you want it."

I signed the necessary paperwork. "Can our sisters come in now?"

"Sure, I'll send them in. I want you to know the Pitocin will be dripping in at a very slow pace. I'll gradually be increasing it throughout the morning."

The girls came in and made themselves as comfortable as they could in the chairs that were provided for them. I don't think they cared about comfort, they were just happy to be there. Gene sat next to me holding my hand. "Hey, did I tell you about Jeff from the firehouse? You know he works for Blackstone Fireworks. He's setting fireworks off in the city. It's going to be televised. He wanted me to tell you that he would be setting some off in honor of our baby tonight."

"Awww, that's so awesome," Tess said

Mary smiled. "What time will they be on?"

"I think they start at 8:00 and end at 10:00."

"Well, at the speed the Pitocin is going in, I hope the baby is here by that time."

"No worries." Gene pointed to the TV. "There's a TV in here."

"I was being sarcastic, sorry. Seriously, though. I do hope the baby is here by then!"

By 11:00 a.m. I was really starting to feel the contractions; they were about every ten minutes. Tess came over to rub my back. "How are you doing, Jane?"

"They hurt, but I'm okay."

"Why don't you try to sleep in between?"

"I want to see Gracie and Kathleen before it gets bad."

"I just spoke to Kathy; they're a few minutes away."

"Okay. Why don't you and Mary go take a break? It's almost lunch time. All of you should go, you too Gene."

"I'm not going anywhere," he said with authority.

"Look, it's going to be a long day, I'm going to need you soon enough. Now, go have something to eat. For me?"

"Yeah, yeah, okay. Girls, are you coming with me?"

"How about you two go, and I'll stay with Jane?" Tess asked. They agreed.

Grace, Kathleen, Kathy, and Marge walked in moments later.

"Hey, baby." Marge looked happy but sympathetic.

"Hey, Mommy" Grace kissed me, the rest followed.

"Are you okay, Mommy?"

"I'm fine, really, I'm doing good. It won't be long now; the contractions are getting closer and more intense. I'm actually having one right now."

You could hear the baby's heart beat speed up over the monitor as the contractions peaked. I felt a tremendous amount of pain, and by looking at everyone's faces I could see that they saw my pain. I did my breathing through it. When the contraction was over I did a cleansing breath, and looked over at Gracie and Kathleen. "Hey girls, I want you here with me in the worst way, but I don't want you to see me like this." Kathy was rubbing my foot sympathetically.

They all nodded in agreement. "Why don't all of you search Dad and Aunt Mary out, they went to get something to eat. You too, Tess. I promise I'll be okay."

"Are you sure, baby?" Marge asked. "I'll stay with you."

"Thanks, I'm sure. I think I'd like to sleep in between these pains. I'll see you guys soon, okay? Really, I'm fine."

All of them walked out of the room looking defeated. I felt a little relieved; I hated the idea of everyone seeing me in pain. I was able to sleep in between my contractions, but the distance between them was getting shorter, and the pain more severe. My coaches were all back in my room within the hour. They all knew when I was contracting. They could hear it on the heart monitor. With each one, they would all look at me.

Gene would say things like, "Oh, that was a good one," or "oh, that wasn't as strong as the last."

I wanted to scream, "How would you know if it was a good one or not?" Then someone would say "You are doing so well, Jane." Again, I just wanted to shout, "SHUT UP." There is something about being in labor, especially toward the end. All thoughts of manners seem to fly out the window. I eventually I turned my back to them...how rude of me. After all, they were just trying to help.

"I need the doctor. I want the epidural."

"Are you sure, Jane?" Gene asked.

"Do I look like I'm sure?"

"Okay, okay, I'll get him."

Dr. Williams moseyed in and examined me.

"You're progressing, but you're only 3.5 centimeters. We can't give you the epidural until you are 4."

"When I'm 4 it will be too late, I've gone from 4 to 10 centimeters in a matter of minutes every time. Please, I know I'm really close."

"Okay, well, the anesthesiologist isn't here right now, but we'll call for him. He can probably be here in a half-hour."

"In half an hour?" I cried.

"Yes, half an hour."

"I guess I don't have a choice," I said to him in a nasty tone.

I would say that last half-hour was one of the longest of my life. Finally he showed up.

"Hi, Mrs. Spiotta, I'm Dr. Smith."

" Yeah, hi. Can you please give me the epidural, I'm about to have this baby!"

"Are you sure you want to have the epidural, if you feel that close to giving birth?"

"Yes, I'm sure."

He told me to sit up, as he couldn't insert the needle into my spine while I was lying down. It was important for me to be still while he inserted it, which was difficult with the amount of pain I was in, but I managed. Within three minutes the agony had left me. I lay back down on the bed. I could feel my abdomen tightening but felt absolutely no pain. At that point Kath came in to see me, and the nurse came in to check my I.V.

"I feel another contraction coming." I smiled as Tess took a picture. I think my smile must have turned to a look of astonishment.

"What's wrong?" Kathy asked.

"Oh no, I feel like I have to push!"

"Honey," the nurse said, "it's just pressure, there is no way, the doctor just checked you."

"Oh yes, there is, I have to push!"

"Believe her, she knows," Kathy said, and then quickly made her escape..

The nurse checked me. "Oh my goodness, you are crowning." She left the room and retrieved the doctor and a few more nurses. One wheeled in a crib. Dr. Williams was masked and ready to deliver our baby. With my legs in stirrups I pushed three times, and out came Thomas. I don't remember much at that moment. I remember hearing a baby crying, and seeing our sisters crying. I also recall feeling a tremendous amount of fear to even lay eyes on him. I'm not proud of that, but that's how I felt. Tess shared with me that she recalls looking at both of us. She said we were looking over at the doctor checking the baby, and seeing the fear of God in our faces. Had I only known then what I know now. There was no need to fear.

A nurse brought Thomas over to us. He was wrapped up in a blanket. Immediately they let the children in to see him. He was so tiny, only five pounds, five ounces. He had pink skin, a tiny nose and mouth, and eyes that were almost vertical. There was no question that he had Down syndrome. Anxiety consumed me. Grace cried, and I held my tears in until she wasn't around. Everyone left the room, and I lost it for the hundredth time since our journey began. Eventually I was brought back to the room in the maternity ward. I happily welcomed the friends and family that came to visit. While some of them were visiting, a nurse came in and said that Thomas would have to be put into I.C.U.

"What's wrong?" Gene asked.

"He's doing well, no worries. His blood sugar is a little low; it's just precautionary. Everything else looks good."

When our evening guests came to visit (my brothers,

sisters-in-law, aunts and even cousins), we all walked down
to the I.C.U. to see him. They all commented on how beautiful
he was, while I went in to try to feed him. Now, that was
overwhelming. He couldn't get any suction on the bottle, the
formula was pouring out of the side of his mouth. I handed
Thomas to the nurse and said "I can't do this." I know it
was rude, but I left my guests and Gene in the hallway, and
went back to my room. I needed to be alone. I knew they all
understood, or at least wanted to.

Gene was back at my room by 8:00 p.m. when visiting
hours were over. I felt awful about leaving everyone, and had
wished I could have handled it better. It was what it was, and
what was done was done. Gene held me while I cried. He
cried some, too. I looked up to see that it was 9:00 p.m. and
said, "The fireworks!"

I found the TV remote control that was attached to my
bed, turned it on, and began to go through the channels. There
they were, beautiful fireworks being displayed over the Cities
Bridge. Gene and I looked at each other, stunned. The song
playing in the background was none other than "You'll Be in
My Heart" by Phil Collins. Coincidence maybe, but we didn't
think so.

Thomas was kept in the I.C.U. the first night, which gave
me the opportunity to sleep straight through. Exhausted
as any mother was after giving birth, I needed the sleep.
Naturally, I felt a little better physically and emotionally the
next day. Having a hot shower helped, of course. Later that
afternoon they released Thomas from I.C.U. and brought him
to me. They placed his crib next to my bed. I was alone with
him. I picked him up out of the crib and unwrapped him
from his blanket, and began examining him, as I did my other
babies. Ten fingers, ten toes, beautiful soft pink skin. He was
precious. Looking at him, I thought of all of the things that
could have been wrong with him medically. I had to and did
feel blessed at that moment. I fed him a bottle. It went a little
bit smoother than the night before. The formula still dripped
out of his mouth, but I felt confident that he got at least some
of it. Before placing him back in his crib, I changed his diaper
and sopping wet undershirt, kissed his little cheek, and placed

him back in his crib. I believe that is when the bonding process had finally begun.

Visitors came and went. Paul and Grace spent a good part of the day with us, taking turns holding Thomas. All was well. That is, until everyone left. I was supposed to have a private room because of my circumstances, but I didn't. That evening they wheeled a girl in who had just given birth to a perfect baby boy. She had several guests in the room. Even though it was late, they were all laughing and chatting, and her phone kept ringing for what seemed like every two minutes. I was so angry, not that she had a healthy baby, but because she was so elated, and although I started to feel a bit of peace, I wasn't elated and wanted to be, too. I remember leaving the room in haste. When I got into the hallway I slid down the wall and a mini meltdown, then I walked down to an empty waiting room and melted some more. I'm happy to say, with the exception of some tears of frustration for Thomas's own struggles, those were the last of the tears I cried for myself.

We pulled up to our house the next day to a huge wooden stork standing on our front lawn. It said, "IT'S A BOY… THOMAS WILLIAM 5lbs, 5oz. 7/4/00". Marge did that for us. I thought it was great. Paul and Grace were standing by the door beaming with excitement. At that moment, when Paul and Grace would argue over who was going to hold him first, I knew I was home, and also knew all would be well… again.

Six Years Later

My entire family, including my siblings, their children, grandchildren and entire extended family were gathered in our yard ready to watch our first annual talent show. It was taking place at our family reunion, which of course wasn't our first. With about 100 pairs of eyes watching, Thomas came out of the house with his au pair Kira, and took center stage on our deck. He was wearing a hula skirt. Kira squatted next to him wearing a hand-made mask over her face. Grace turned the stereo on, and that is when that precious voice began to sing "You'll Be in My Heart," which he clearly directed at Tess, reaching his arms out to us as he sang. I'm filling up writing this because he is my gift, my amazing little boy. Needless to say, there wasn't a dry eye in the house. It was a moment that stood still in time, for me and for the rest of my family. I didn't know Kira and Tommy had been practicing for weeks. I'm eternally grateful to them and to God for those amazing moments.

That September Evening 2006

A knock on the bathroom door stirred me. "Jane, it's 7:30, don't you want to put Tommy to bed, or do you want me to do it?" Gene shouted through the door. "You've been in there for over an hour."

At that point the water was ice cold, I must have fallen asleep. "Sorry, I'll be right out." I stepped out of the bath, dried off and quickly put my PJs on. When I came out of the bathroom, Tommy and I walked up the stairs and into his room. I stroked his thick blond hair as we prayed, and then I sang him his favorite songs until he drifted off to sleep.

By 8:00 a.m. Grace had left for school, she was in her sophomore year. I got Tommy ready for his first day of first grade. He looked so handsome dressed in his new blue jeans, a white button down oxford shirt, and his penny loafers that were just like Grandpa's. His blonde hair was cut surfer style, and his blue eyes were as blue as Grace's, with the same amount of sparkle. We arrived at his school—he was so proud to wear his backpack. He held my hand as we walked down the hallway to his classroom. "Room 212, here it is, Tommy."

We entered the room. A dark-haired girl in her late twenties stood behind the desk. Looking at the name tag he was wearing she said, "You must be Thomas." They smiled at each other. That was when I noticed a vase that stood on her desk holding a single silk rose.

To be continued…

9771994R0012

Made in the USA
Charleston, SC
12 October 2011